Pass your exams

brilliantideas

one good idea can change your life...

Pass your exams

Study skills for success

Andrew Holmes

CAREFUL NOW

Short of outright cheating (risky), or bribing the examiner (expensive), there is no way of ensuring 100% guaranteed success in an exam. What this book does is offer brilliant ideas for putting in your best performance on the day, when it counts. That means making the most of your biggest asset – you. What it doesn't mean is doing your job for you. You alone are in the hot seat on the big day. Nobody else – not us, not the author, not your mum – is responsible for the outcome. We can't sit your exam for you, and no book is going to be a substitute for knowing your stuff. We've given you weapons-grade advice for passing whatever tests come your way but only the snake oil salesmen will guarantee success. So the best of luck, we have our fingers crossed for you, but don't blame us if it doesn't work out this time.

Copyright © The Infinite Ideas Company Limited, 2005

The right of Andrew Holmes to be identified as the author of this book has been asserted in accordance with the Copyright, Designs and Patents Act 1988

First published in 2005 by
The Infinite Ideas Company Limited
36 St Giles
Oxford
OX1 3LD
United Kingdom
www.infideas.com

A CIP catalogue record for this book is available from the British Library.

ISBN 1-904902-29-4

Brand and product names are trademarks or registered trademarks of their respective owners.

Designed and typeset by Baseline Arts Ltd, Oxford
Printed and bound by TJ International, Cornwall

Brilliant ideas

Brilliant features

Each chapter of this book is designed to provide you with an inspirational idea that you can read quickly and put into practice straight away.

Throughout you'll find four features that will help you get right to the heart of the idea:

- *Here's an idea for you* Take it on board and give it a go – right here, right now. Get an idea of how well you're doing so far.

- *Try another idea* If this idea looks like a life-changer then there's no time to lose. *Try another idea* will point you straight to a related tip to enhance and expand on the first.

- *Defining ideas* Words of wisdom from masters and mistresses of the art, plus some interesting hangers-on.

- *How did it go?* If at first you do succeed, try to hide your amazement. If, on the other hand, you don't, then this is where you'll find a Q and A that highlights common problems and how to get over them.

Introduction

Ask yourself the following...

- Do you want to be more confident in the exam hall?

- Do you need to be much more motivated to study?

- Are you lost for ideas on how to improve your study and exam technique?

- Are you looking for ways to focus and even reduce the amount of revision you need to do?

- Are you seeking some hints and tips to make life a little easier?

So you've finally got around to studying for your exams. It's about time!

You've dug out your notes, picked up a few books from the library and have even got hold of a few past papers. You sit there staring at the huge pile of material you've got to go through, thinking 'Where do I start?' and then look for something else to do – anything, so long as it's not studying. You know, make a cup of tea, find some job around the house that you have been meaning to complete for months, if not years, watch television, ring up a mate or anything else that comes to mind. You're bored, fed up and can't face the prospect of spending hours, days, weeks or even months studying. The problem is you haven't got much choice.

This is where this book comes in. It's not written by an academic or a professor sitting in an ivory tower. Instead, it's written by someone who has spent his life taking one kind of exam or other. Like you, I can't escape them; and like you, I have to pass them.

I started off as an average student with middle-of-the-road grades; nothing earth-shatteringly great, but not bad either. But as time wore on, I got tired of having to work so hard to get okay grades. I didn't necessarily want to be a spoddy swot with straight As, but I did want a better return on my investment. So I embarked on a journey to pick up as many techniques and ideas as I could that would (a) reduce my workload and (b) make me more successful. As I passed from one rung of the exam ladder to the next, I found that my grades gradually improved, so that, by the time I completed my Masters degree, I walked away with a distinction. The other thing I needed to do was to avoid all the stress. This wasn't the stress you get from parents or teachers, which I know some of you face, especially when you can't be bothered to work for your exams. No, this was from the fear of failure and the burning desire to pass. I certainly didn't want the ignominy of retakes; and taking exams once is more than enough for most people, including me. The problem was that I got so stressed out and obsessed about my exams that everything else took a back seat. I was a grumpy student who did nothing but pace up and down with a frown on my face. This had to change. So I also took time to figure out how to reduce my levels of stress and increase my confidence, both of which were vital to becoming more successful in my study and, of course, in my exams. I spoke to the cool students who were never fazed, I looked into all those cheesy self-help, clap-happy books written by over-the-top, white-toothed gurus and above all I looked at what drove me crazy about exams. Over time I lost my fear of exams and actually started to enjoy them. This created a virtuous circle in which I was more motivated to study, looked forward to my exams and, above all, remained calm and confident. It also helped to raise my grades.

Once all the formal and academic stuff had finished, I still faced other exams and tests; professional exams to demonstrate that I was competent enough to undertake certain jobs and tests at the end of vocational courses to show that I had learnt something. These were different from my academic exams, but my kitbag of techniques, skills and attitudes that I built up over the years helped me then and helps me now.

When I was asked to write this I thought great, at last I have a chance to impart an average guy's exam techniques to all those students out there who are struggling just as I did. So this book is here to save each and every one of you the time-consuming task of figuring it out for yourself. I wanted to give you a mix of things to help you. Sure, it's great if you can work out how to do better in a multiple choice exam, but I think being successful at studying and exams is more than that. It's about attitude, it's about tackling the process of committing all that information into your brain and it's about learning how to learn. Above all, it's about being able to pass exams. So this book is not just about technique, it's about the way you think about study and exams, and about improving how you tackle them. It could change your life…literally.

No matter what you are studying or what type of exam you are expecting to sit, there is help beyond this page. If this is the first or even the last time you will be taking exams, you'll find hints and tips that will get you through. Becoming competent at studying is one thing; enjoying it is another. I can't promise you that, but at least it should make it a bit more bearable.

Oh, and by the way, you'll still have to sit the exam. I can't do that for you.

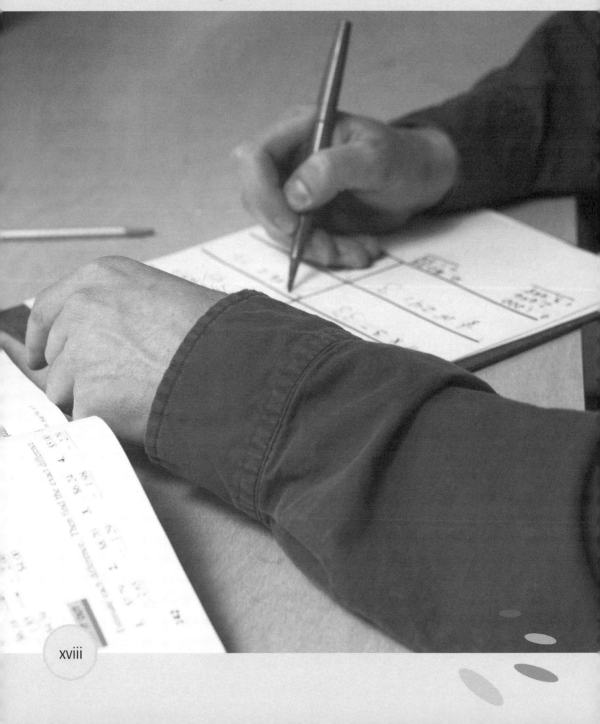

1

Are you sitting comfortably?

If you're coming back into the study and exam thing after a few years off (for good behaviour), it's a good idea to refresh yourself with what works and what doesn't.

Most people think they're leaving study and exams behind when they leave school or university, but return to it later in their working life or even in retirement. The need to gain more qualifications means that it's time to refresh those study and exam skills.

If it's been a while since you followed any kind of formal study or taken exams, then it's important to remind yourself of the pitfalls you should avoid and the skills you need to have at your disposal before you get cracking. Studying and taking exams is not like learning to ride a bike. Once you have ridden a bicycle you remember it forever, but with studying you seem to get out of practice, and it takes a while to get the skills and discipline back. So here are the things to look out for:

■ Never knowing where to start. If it's been a while, you can be easily overwhelmed with what you have to do and as a result will allow yourself to be distracted.

Here's an idea for you... **Returning to study can be difficult, so in order to get the most out of it, complete a learning styles questionnaire (freely available on the internet) before you start.**

■ Poor time management. With a heavy workload it can be easy to lose control over what assignment has to be in when.

■ Boredom. All the reasons why you vowed never to study ever again all those years ago haven't gone away. And when you begin studying again, they all come flooding back: dry lectures, dull subjects, difficult assignments – and of course those dreaded exams!

■ Getting stuff to sink in. Locking the information you need to retain for the exams in your long-term memory is probably one skill you've managed to lose. It's important you re-learn some of those skills that stood you in good stead at school or university.

■ Understanding what the subject is really about. If anything, this is the least of your worries (well I hope it is), because as you get older your ability to question and hence understand what's told to you is far better than when you were young and took things at face value.

■ Coping with the volume of material. This is often the hardest thing to get back into, given that life beyond study rarely throws up such requirements.

Thankfully many of the techniques I have used over the years will provide you with the antidote to the horrors of studying and exams.

As well as avoiding the pitfalls, it's a good idea to ask yourself some fairly tough questions to ensure you are ready for the challenges ahead. The questions I always ask myself when I am going to follow a major course are:

■ What are my motivations for undertaking this course/programme? These could be work related, such as promotion or the need to enhance your technical knowledge, general interest or general advancement. Understanding the answer to this question will help you set your personal goals and maintain your motivation.

Returning to studying in order to complete your vocational training or to secure your next promotion? If so, dip into IDEA 51, *Vocation, vocation.*

Try another idea...

■ How good are my time management and prioritisation skills? I'm afraid that these are very important if you're going to be able to deal with the workload.

■ What study techniques am I familiar with and what ones do I need to learn? There is no harm in trying to resurrect what worked for you in the past and then augmenting these with some additional techniques.

■ How important is it that I pass? For some people, it's the process of learning that really matters. For others, it will be passing and for others still, it will be excelling. The answer to this question lies in the answer to the first one (why you are doing it in the first place).

■ What kinds of things could get in the way of your study (home, work, social life, etc.)? Unless you are single and have decided to have a year out to take an MBA, those returning to study tend to have other priorities which they need to balance. Rest assured it can be done, but it is not always easy (I completed my Masters whilst continuing with my day job and helping my wife look after my three-month-old son; not easy, I can assure you).

'I'll be back.'
ARNOLD SCHWARZENEGGER

Defining idea...

■ How good are your studying habits? It's worth reviewing what your habits were like when you were in full-time education. If they were good, then you should fall into them quite easily. But if you had bad habits, then you will need to set new ones (good ones, that is, not bad!).

Q   It all seems a bit too hard. Am I wise going back to studying?

A   *All studying is hard to some degree or other, and questioning whether it is worthwhile is very common. Understanding why you have decided to study again is important as this both allows to you to set your goals and also ensures you have something to motivate you. If you can keep interested you should have a lot of fun along the way. So yes, you are probably wise.*

Q   Where can I get the advice I need to help understand what's expected of me?

A   *All courses should provide you with some information about the effort and time requirements expected of you. Many courses, and especially those which lead to higher degrees, will require you to attend an interview and often give you the chance to attend a briefing session on the course, its contents and the demands that will be made upon you. These are very helpful and will guide you on what you will be doing over the coming months or years.*

2

Syllabus savvy

The syllabus serves an important purpose: it tells us what we are meant to learn. Of course, it also tells the teachers what they should be teaching us, which helps.

Armed with a syllabus, you are unbeatable. No excuses about not knowing, no misunderstandings of what's expected of you. In fact, if you read it, understand it and use it, you ought to do pretty well.

During our English classes many, many moons ago, we would sit down whilst our teacher, Mr X (not his real name), would read us stories. He was such a great narrator that we all sat there thinking that the course was a bit of a breeze, as we didn't actually have to do anything. Three-quarters of the way through the first year, we changed teacher. This is when we got the shock of our lives: we were a little more than a year away from our exam and we hadn't covered any of the syllabus. Boy, did we have to work hard. This taught me two lessons. The first is the need to be wary of any teacher who would rather read you stories than teach, and second, make sure you know the syllabus. Although many tutors don't outline the syllabus in great detail, you should be relieved to know that the examination boards

Here's an idea for you... **Get hold of the syllabus for each of the subjects you are studying. Once you have got them, keep them in a file along with key notes, past exam papers and anything else you need. As you complete your course, check it against the syllabus and tick off the parts you have covered. If any ticks are missing at the end of the course, bring it to your teacher's attention.**

do. Looking at a random example of a syllabus, I noted that it gives you some very useful information, including:

■ The aims of the course – in other words, what they are trying to get you to learn. In many cases it is much more than the guts of the subject. For example, my randomly chosen syllabus included the selection, organisation and presentation of information as one of its aims.

■ What is expected of the students in terms of the skills they will be expected to demonstrate. These are often very specific and once again are not completely focused on the subject matter itself but are aimed at testing such things as a student's ability to investigate and communicate.

■ How the student's knowledge will be tested (written exams, modular tests, multiple choice tests and coursework) and the percentage split between the various forms of assessment.

■ A detailed outline of the course, including some of the major facts/knowledge the student is expected to understand, and what is expected of the student in terms of what they need to demonstrate for each part of the syllabus.

■ An outline of what the coursework is designed to achieve, what skills the student should be demonstrating whilst completing the coursework and how the marks will be awarded.

- Some information about grading, re-sitting exams and so on, plus a description of what the grades mean.

Some of the simplest exams to master are multiple choice. Choosing IDEA 45, *It's as simple as a, b, c*, will show you how.

Try another idea...

So, the syllabus provides you with a wealth of information that helps you in your studying and revision. Here are some of the ways using a syllabus has helped me. It allowed me to understand the bigger picture of the subjects I was studying. Rather than being on a magical mystery tour, with my tutor in the driving seat, I was thus able to get a complete view of what I would be studying at the start of the course. This was great because I could then track my progress. It was also invaluable when it came to revision and exam preparation: by outlining the assessment objectives and how this assessment was to take place, I knew what was expected of me. The syllabus was also very helpful during my revision planning because it kept me on track and ensured that my plan was comprehensive and covered the entire subject area. Another way in which it helped me during the revision itself was by enabling me to check that my answers had demonstrated the key knowledge the examiners were expecting to see. If they did, I knew that I had grasped the subject. If they didn't, I knew I still had some more work to do.

Armed with this information, I did pretty well – and so should you. So use the syllabus to:

'I came, I saw, I conquered.'
JULIUS CAESAR

Defining idea...

- Familiarise yourself with the content of the subject.

- Understand what's expected by the examiners and what they will be looking for.

- Ensure your revision plan covers everything you need to know.

■ Refer back to when you have made your revision notes to make sure they are complete.

■ Check your answers to sample questions in order to clarify that you know your stuff.

Be warned, though: the syllabus can be a very long and incredibly dry document!

How did it go?

Q   Where is the best place to get hold of a syllabus?

A   *You can get a copy from your examination board. These days you should be able to print them off from the board's website. Alternatively, they will sell you a paper copy; it's cheap, honest and well worth the money.*

Q   What if the syllabus has changed?

A   *Good point: examiners do have to change the syllabus from time to time to keep up with the latest thinking on the subject. However, changes are usually planned quite a long way in advance so that disruption is kept to a minimum. Let's face it: if your course takes two years to complete, it is unlikely that the syllabus will change midway through. So you rarely have to worry about a change, as it only occurs at the beginning.*

3
It's all about attitude, dude

You can't escape the need to study, whether it's for your entry level qualifications, degree, postgraduate or professional exams. To master the art requires discipline and persistence – and attitude.

The attitude you have towards study will ultimately define the attitudes and behaviours you bring into the workplace and your life in general, so it's a good idea to suss them out sooner rather than later and correct them if you need to.

Experiments with young children have shown that the delaying of gratification puts them in good stead for their future lives (for a start, it gives them something to look forward to). The research involved offering the children some sweets. The amount they were offered varied according to how long they were willing to wait before they ate them. Those who waited longer got more than those who dived straight in. The children were then tracked well into adulthood and it was found that the kids who were willing to wait longer for their sweets were more successful than those who weren't. Their future success lay in their ability to delay gratification. It's possible they also had better sex lives, but the experiments didn't show this.

Here's an idea for you...

Take a little time out and go somewhere quiet and away from distraction. On a piece of paper answer the following questions: What do you like about studying? What do you dislike about studying? What could you do to make the process of studying more enjoyable? What sort of environment do you need to make your study more productive? What resources could you utilise to make your study more effective? By answering these questions honestly, you'll have the basis for understanding your attitude to study and, more importantly, what you can do to make it a better experience for you.

Another experiment, this time with students, involved asking them what they wanted to achieve in their lives once they had graduated. As expected, most wanted to go on to great things, have fantastic careers and so on. They were also tracked throughout their adult lives. The successful ones had made a list of their life goals and used it to guide their decisions; the unsuccessful ones hadn't bothered to keep a list and so bumbled along with the rest of us.

So how does this help us with studying? Well, first, it highlights the need to keep distractions to a minimum. For example, say it's a Friday night after a long week. What would you rather do: study or go out with your mates? The latter option might be more fun, but unfortunately the best option is the first one. This is not to say you shouldn't have any fun, but you are far better off building it into your study timetable – or delaying gratification, like in the experiments above. Secondly, it illustrates how some basic personal discipline sets you along the right path towards success. And finally, I think it identifies the need to take a long, hard look at how you feel about studying and why you don't like it (if, of course, you don't). You may find it is due to the environment in which you are studying, or it could be because the approach you are taking is not tuned into the way you like to work. Whatever the underlying reasons, it is well worth figuring out how you can have an attitude that allows you to succeed.

Consider Roger Bannister. Before he ran the four-minute mile, the medical profession believed that it was impossible, and those who attempted it would literally drop dead. Roger overcame these barriers by developing a winning attitude in which he imagined himself breaking that elusive four minutes.

Attitude is all in the mind, so if you want to create a winning attitude to study then sprint over to IDEA 33, *Breaking the four-minute mile.*

Try another idea...

Of course, attitude also extends to how you feel about exams. Reflecting on the types of attitudes about exams suggests that people fall into one of three camps. The first comprises people who are petrified by exams and the very word puts the fear of God into them. These are the students who tend to panic and get flustered at the slightest problem, and no matter how well prepared they are, they can still fail because their nerves get the better of them. Next are the students who don't care about exams and, quite frankly, aren't worried if they pass or fail. I always find this an odd behaviour, as if you can't be bothered, why enter them in the first place? I also know that it is precisely these students who end up regretting this attitude later in life when they have a dull and uninteresting working life. Finally, there are those who are supremely confident and enjoy taking exams. Now you may dislike them, but you have to admit they tend to do better than most. I know which one I'd rather be!

'Pleasure in the job puts perfection in the work.'
ARISTOTLE

Defining idea...

11

How did it go?

Q   The very thought of study turns me off. How can I deal with it?

A   *Well, studying can be boring, feel pointless at times and seem endless. But it can equally be fun, stimulating, fruitful and targeted. Key to making it the latter rather than the former is to work out how to make studying work for you. So think about how you can do this and make a few attitudinal changes, and you'll be fine.*

Q   Where can I get help if I need it?

A   *If you still need some help developing the right attitude, why not seek out advice from your fellow students or perhaps the tutors. They might have some additional tools and techniques which will help you.*

4

Protect your environment

Where do you like to get down to it? Do you prefer a soundtrack or would you rather do it in silence? How you create your perfect study environment is up to you.

I am a difficult person to please when it comes to studying: it's got to be total silence or...well, total silence. I get terribly crotchety if there is any noise, because I get so easily distracted.

If you can't get your environment right then it can ruin your concentration and the effectiveness of your study. However, we are taught at an early age that the best place to study is confined to your room, well away from any other human contact. The point is, though, that this doesn't necessarily work for everyone. There are two problems with this model of study. First, too many of us are sent to our room when we are or have been naughty, which means we associate our room with punishment – not the most conducive environment in which to study. Secondly, if we find that being in our room is the last place we want to focus on books, exams and learning,

Here's an idea for you...

Create a list of the things you need to be in place for your study environment to be as productive as possible. Consider such things as noise, light, heat, and access to computers and the internet. Use this to tailor your environment so that distractions are minimised.

it sets up behavioural patterns which stay with us throughout our academic career.

Sussing out what works for you should not be too much of a burden. The best way is to try out different approaches. So, start by having total silence – it's what you were taught, and as good a place to start as any. If this doesn't work, perhaps it's because you need a little bit of background noise, so pop on a CD or tape of some of your favourite music. It is well known that music stimulates the brain by causing it to look for patterns and a sense of order in the song you are listening to. So as you are listening, your brain is working furiously to work out whether the melodies you are hearing are the same or different. The best music is one that has a 4/4 beat, so stuff like reggae and rap are good, but dance music isn't. If concentration still eludes you, you could try a complete change of scene, like a different room, or a public or college library or even a park (weather permitting). Whenever I am studying, I often ask if I can use a friend's house because it provides less distraction and forces me to focus. I find it terribly difficult to study at home because there are too many other things to interest me, like food, the kids, the garden...well, almost anything.

Location is only one part of your environment – the external part. What you consume also affects how productive you are. Here are some tips which you might want to consider:

- Avoid all chemicals that are toxic to the brain, like drugs, nicotine, excessive caffeine and alcohol. So studying in Starbucks or a local bar may not be the best place after all.

If you can't find anywhere that works for you, why not seek out the company of others and join a study group, as suggested in IDEA 22, *Many hands make light work*.

Try another idea...

- Keep your salt intake low, because too much salt depresses brain function. Salt intake increases blood pressure, and high blood pressure can harm memory, attention span and reasoning.

- Don't eat processed food, as much of this contains what is known as trans fats. These are also known as 'brain drainers' because of the way they disrupt the messages between neural pathways.

- Get plenty of protein and vitamin B, as these help to keep your brain active. They do this by stimulating the release of dopamine. It's also a good idea to have plenty of oily fish. This may seem like an old wives' tale, but it really is brain food (it's the omega-3 polyunsaturated fatty acids, for those of you who are interested).

In the end, creating the perfect study environment requires you to think outside of the box. And once you've found that perfect combination, you'll be in great shape for focused, productive studying.

'Success is the good fortune that comes from aspiration, desperation, perspiration and inspiration.'
EVAN ESAR, American humorist

Defining idea...

15

How did it go?

Q   What if the slightest noise distracts me?

A   *You too? I suffered for years with this, as no matter how small the noise I was distracted and my concentration was lost. Why not try the earplugs you can get for long haul flights? They are great because they cut out all but the loudest of noises. With these firmly implanted in your ears, nothing should disturb you. Another thing to use is white noise headphones. These cut out external sound entirely, which means you'll only have your inner voice disturbing you.*

Q   What if I can't find the best environment?

A   *Perhaps you are trying too hard. Maybe a combination of things might help, or you might need to persevere a little bit longer. Trouble is, there is always something more fun to do than study. A good idea is to limit your study to short bursts of between 30 and 45 minutes followed by breaks of a similar period.*

5

Charting your success

When it comes to study, maintaining your motivation is difficult at the best of times. So how do you do it? One thing that seems to work for a lot of people is the use of a study charter.

I came across the concept of a classroom charter when I was discussing it with a teacher friend of mine. The charter is designed to improve discipline, self-esteem and above all learning, and it seems to work too.

I have thought long and hard, during my many forays into the world of study, about how to keep my motivation levels as high as they need to be. I have tried literally dozens of techniques. In every case they have helped to improve my enthusiasm to buckle down and study. But the most effective to date has been the use of a 'study charter', as I call it. I borrowed the idea from enlightened teachers who use it to good effect in their classrooms. Some of the ideas behind classroom charters provide an insight into their value. Because they are co-developed with the students, they create a collaborative environment where discipline is improved and learning is enhanced. It also sets clear expectations about what gets rewarded and what gets punished. So I thought what's good for the goose should be good for the

---

Here's an idea for you...

Using the headings 'Rules for general study', 'How you intend to interact with your tutors', 'Rules for revising', 'Rewards you will give yourself for good studying behaviour', 'Sanctions for not following the rules you set out', produce your own study charter. When you are creating it, think carefully about how to make it work for you. Once you have built it and tried it out for a few weeks, reassess it and, if necessary, tweak it so that it works better.

Defining idea...

'The classroom charter gives pupils responsibility. Not only must they come up with a workable set of rules, rewards and sanctions, they must keep to them.'
IAN HEDLEY

gander, although I thought the punishment bit was rather harsh (well, for some people at least!). So, after some careful thought and some lengthy discussions with students at all stages of their academic careers, I came up with the following headings for my study charter:

■ *Rules for general study*, which should include making sure you complete assignments on time and to the best of your abilities, attending all classes, lectures, practicals and seminars, etc.

■ *How you intend to interact with your tutors*, which should include asking for help when you need it and being willing to raise questions in lectures.

■ *Rules for revising*, which should include when you will study, how long you will work before taking a break, any strategies you prefer to use, and so on.

■ *Rewards you will give yourself for good studying behaviour*, which could include nights off, trips to the cinema or pub, and so on.

■ *Sanctions for not following the rules you set out.* These should be personal to you and ideally have some kind of impact. So it might be ruling out that trip to the cinema, for example.

The purpose behind having such a charter is to keep yourself disciplined and committed to your study and revision regime. Having used charters a few times now, I can recommend them; I even believe they improved my grades. Here's a recent example.

Studying is not just about putting up a study charter; you also need to ensure that your study environment is conducive to success. Check this out in IDEA 4, *Protect your environment*.

Try another idea...

Learning Charter – Masters

Study rules
- To take every opportunity to advance my understanding of the subjects in my course by attending all lectures, seminars and tutorials
- To make effective use of the library and to spend five hours a week studying there
- To complete all my assignments to the best of my ability and to hand them in on time

Interaction with tutors and fellow students
- To seek feedback from tutors and to ask for help and advice when I need it
- To work with my fellow students and take every opportunity to learn from them

Revision rules
- To create and work to a revision timetable which starts at least six weeks before the exams
- To revise for five hours every day, one hour at a time, with a 45-minute break between sessions
- To use mind mapping, key words and memory stacks as my primary techniques
- To have weekly revision sessions with some of my fellow students
- To undertake a mock exam every week using past papers
- To extend my knowledge of the subject by reading the latest books and journals

Rewards
- All weekends should be free of revision
- Once a week go to the cinema
- Two nights per week go out for a drink with my friends

Sanctions
- If I don't fulful my study commitments the time will be made up during the weekend
- If I don't follow my timetable, I will cancel one of the rewards (cinema, night out etc.)

It's important that, once you have created your charter, you place it somewhere prominent. One option would be to get it converted to a poster and stick it on the wall in the place you have designated as your study. There, it will act as your guardian angel, watching over you and making sure you stick to your guns. And, because you will have built in some rewards, it won't be all work and no play.

How did it go?

Q   When should I create my study charter?

A   *The best time to create it is at the beginning of your next major study period. Do this before you start any course, as in order for it to have the best effect it needs to cover the learning as well as revising part of the process.*

Q   Do you think it would work in a group environment?

A   *As the idea came from a classroom environment, it ought to. I would produce one for your group study sessions if you intend to use them as part of your exam preparation. I would also use them for group exercises. This helps the group to agree a common set of rules which they will follow and is the perfect way to iron out any differences of opinion before they disrupt the productivity of the group.*

Q   When should I update it?

A   *There are two occasions when you ought to think about updating your charter. The first is if it isn't working and the second is when you commence a new course. So if you used one whilst at school, you would probably need to create a new one when you go to university. And if you are pursuing a vocational course you should adjust it to take into account the difference between these courses and academic ones you have taken in the past, as well as your home circumstances.*

6
On your marks

You have spent up to three years learning your subject, weeks or months revising and a few hours regurgitating all that knowledge in the exam hall. That's exhausting stuff. So how do you feel about those who are going to mark it? Possibly a little apprehensive.

Examiners don't have much time to mark scripts — sometimes only a few minutes each. So if you want to get the best marks possible, you need to understand how to catch their eye.

There's a bit of a paradox with marking exams. On one hand, the scripts are assessed and allocated marks in a very short space of time, and certainly in less time than it took you to write them. But on the other hand, examiners have to follow certain rules themselves which take a little longer to construct than you might think. When you consider what goes on between your walking out after completing the exam and receiving the results, you can see why it takes so long. Once you have handed in your script, the examiners need to ensure that the marking scheme is fair. A number of scripts have been marked in order to confirm that this is so, and that those assessing the papers understand how they will be allocating the marks.

Here's an idea for you... **List all the subjects you are taking exams in and note down three things. First, the grade you would love to get (all As, I'm sure); secondly, the grade you will probably get (being honest, not all As); and thirdly, how you could close the gap between the two.**

Even though the time this process takes can seem an age as you wait for your results, they have your best interests at heart.

You can serve your own best interests by picking up as many marks as possible, and the way to do that is to get into the mind of the examiner and to understand what differentiates an A paper from an F paper. First, here's a quick view of what A–F papers look like:

■ A papers are fluent, well written and display a mastery of the subject. They have a freshness to them either in thinking or in clarity. In other words, they have an edge.

■ B papers display substantial knowledge of the subject, are well written and contain plenty of references to the source material. Their conclusions are solid if unoriginal, and overall the question has been answered competently.

■ C papers are average. They are logical, have a reasonable grasp of the material and come across as okay. Without any real depth of analysis or of the wider assessment of the issues, such papers will never set the world alight.

■ D papers. Hmm, not perfect by any means, but at least the author is familiar with the subject. However, there is often no structure and the thought process comes across as disorganised. So don't expect too many marks.

■ E papers. Could it get much worse? Only a weak appreciation of the subject here, but better than none at all! Couple this with poor structure and analysis, and you are looking at scraping a pass.

To organise your ideas on paper simply and clearly, develop the Minto style of writing, courtesy of IDEA 27, *Night boat to Cairo*.

Try another idea...

■ F papers. A complete cock-up. Badly structured, badly written and normally demonstrating a complete misunderstanding of the question and, indeed, the subject.

So, with that in mind, how do you get the best marks possible? Here are some tips from those who know:

1. Provide a very clear introduction and outline of your argument. If you do this well you could earn quite a few marks, perhaps even 15%.

2. Make sure there is a clear structure to your answer. This separates an A grade paper from a C grade or, worse still, an F grade. You will be awarded marks for a good structure. The best way to achieve this is to make one point per paragraph, keeping each to a Goldilocks length (not too long, not too short – just right).

'Four times, under our educational rules, the human pack is shuffled and cut at eleven-plus, sixteen-plus, eighteen-plus and twenty-plus and happy is he who comes top of the deck on each occasion, but especially the last. This is called Finals, the very name of which implies that nothing of importance can happen after it.'
DAVID LODGE

Defining idea...

3. Ensure that the points you make are supporting the argument you are putting forward. It is always tempting to dump everything you know into the answer, but this often diverts the examiner's eye from all the good stuff.

4. Try to cover everything you need to in the time allotted, so that your paper stacks up, addresses all the issues and includes all the analysis.

5. Include all the content, supporting references, examples and data you need to reinforce your argument. This is where you will pick up at least 25% of your marks.

6. Have a crisp, hard-hitting conclusion to leave the examiner with a lasting impression that you know your stuff. As with the introduction, you will pick up some useful marks – up to 10%, in fact.

7. Write clearly, and ensure your spelling is accurate and your use of grammar is good. It's amazing how you can let yourself down when under time pressure, and examiners are now concerned about it.

So there you have it: all you need to get great marks.

Q If my results are worse than I expected, should I appeal?

A *Every student has the right to appeal against their exam grade. Whether you choose to or not depends on how bad your results are. For example, if you came out of the exam hall after what you thought was a great paper and then end up with a D, it is worth appealing just in case there has been a mix up. Usually when exam papers are re-marked the result is moved by a few percentage points, so if the original mark was borderline, it could make a difference to the grade. Often, though, the overall grade stays the same.*

Q What should I learn from the examiners, then?

A *Quite simply, to focus on the question, make sure your answer is well structured and don't overdo it. You should make it as easy as possible for the examiner to mark your paper. The harder it is, the more likely it is you will lose valuable marks.*

7

Books, glorious books

Some one million books are published every year. Now that's a lot. This means there's plenty of material floating around out there that you can draw on, and what better place to find it all than in a library.

I love books (non-fiction, of course) and have a library at home. Nothing gives me more satisfaction than when my son asks me a question about his homework and I can direct him to one of the books on the shelf.

I think there are two types of people when it comes to studying and books: those who are full on and use books to the max, and those who really can't be bothered and rely on the stuff that is given to them by their tutors. The second group of people are missing out on so much, especially as the former tend to be more successful. Books are great for so many reasons. Some of the most important are the following:

■ There's always the nugget, that killer piece of information that makes the whole process of reading it worthwhile. I always remembering a book entitled *The Argument Culture*, which I was reading for a vocational course on negotiation. The

Here's an idea for you... **Before you next go to the library, make a list of the information you need and questions you need answering (either for your future exam or for your notes). Then, when you arrive, get focused, pick up the books and journals you need and find a big desk. Once you have settled down, take each question in turn and use the available information to secure the key facts you need to answer it. At the end of the session you will have captured the information you needed without having wasted your time.**

book proved to be useful, but the best nugget of all appeared in the last line of the last paragraph. Had I not bothered to read it, I would not have benefited. And no, I'm not going to tell you what it is – you'll just have to read it yourself!

■ They are incredibly interactive, versatile and perhaps irreplaceable as a student's friend. You can underline text, you can use a highlighter pen to highlight paragraphs and images, you can fold down the corners of the pages that matter and you can use this to skip to the key facts and figures without having to leave your chair. And, of course, you can take it anywhere. Just make sure it's your copy, not one you've borrowed from the library.

■ A book often contains everything you need to know about your subject. Credit where credit's due: the author has taken great trouble to scour the latest and greatest information in order to write the thing. And that saves you all the hard work. All you need to do is to read what he or she has written and add it to your own bank of knowledge.

One of the difficulties for anyone studying is to get hold of the books they need. You'd have to be a millionaire to afford all the recommended texts that most courses have on their reading lists. This is where the library comes in handy. They should have multiple copies of the major texts, and plenty of other books besides that will cover the broader aspects of the subject and hence allow you to pick up extra marks when the exam comes round. Libraries don't normally allow you (or your fellow students) to take out the set texts, which means they will normally be available when you are, which is always a bonus. Being in the library also offers up some other advantages, including:

If you really want to get the maximum out of books while avoiding information overload, you'd be wise to check out IDEA 10, *Too much information.*

Try another idea...

- They hold journals and trade publications, which can contain lots of useful and very up-to-date information.

- They are quiet and relatively distraction free, so if you are focused, you can get lots done in a relatively short space of time.

- The sheer volume of books available means that, in the main, you'll find what you need.

'The good of a book lies in its being read.'
UMBERTO ECO

Defining idea...

- They hold past papers and other useful information about the curriculum.

I used to love going into the library with my flatmates at university. The idea behind it was that, in order to get some serious drinking in, we would have to earn it by spending 2–3 hours in the library from late afternoon. Being focused under these circumstances was tricky at times, because we would mess around, but ultimately we got plenty done. And once we'd finished, it was down to the bar for some well-earned liquid refreshment.

Q   **Should I buy all the books I need?**

A   *This is quite tough one. You could buy all the books you need, but the chances are you'll never read them again once you've finished your course, though you could always sell them on. My advice is to buy the core texts (as these always seem to be in short supply in the library) and borrow the rest.*

Q   **I am not a great fan of libraries, so how can I get what I need with the minimum of contact?**

A   *There are two ways. The first is to photocopy the relevant parts of the book (within copyright limits, of course) for use back at home and the second is to consider the use of audio books, which, if available, will provide you with a slimmed-down version of the text, focused on key points only.*

Q   **How do I get the most up-to-date information?**

A   *Not with books, I'm afraid. These are usually at least 12 months out of date because of the time it takes to write, edit, publish and distribute them to the bookshops. The best place to find the latest thinking is to scan the myriad of journals and trade publications. The good thing about the articles and papers that appear in these publications is that they are much shorter than books, are more focused and may well address the question you are looking to answer. And where's the best place to find them? You've guessed it, the library.*

8

Standing on the shoulders of giants

These days there are plenty of study aids available to make your life easier when it comes to study. So why not dig deep and fork out some cash on a few?

When I first started studying, the number and availability of study guides was quite limited. Nowadays, there are even study guides for every conceivable subject and exam. So what's stopping you from using them?

Study guides are not necessarily new, but they are certainly more prevalent these days. They are excellent additions to the studying armoury because they can provide immediate focus to those who don't fancy the hard slog of the swot and are a helpful fillip to those who need to increase their knowledge. Study guides are great for so many reasons:

- They set out the entire syllabus for you, which means you are able to use the guide as the basis for structuring your revision.

Here's an idea for you...

If you feel that study guides are for you but are not sure how to best to use them, then do the following. Create a matrix which lists the topics comprising your study subject from top to bottom and the topics covered in the study guide from left to right. Then colour code how comprehensive the coverage is. I favour a simple red–amber–green system, where green is great (excellent coverage, little more to do), amber is alright (augment the information with some additional sources) and red is rubbish (look elsewhere).

■ They cover every subject in sufficient detail to allow you to pass the exam without any additional input. So, if you are that way inclined, you can probably get by with an average grade without straying from the content of the study guide. Well worth the few pounds you spent on it.

■ They give you plenty of hints and tips about how to approach the specific types of question you might face in the exam, which in itself is very helpful and can help you focus your efforts.

■ They are written by experts in their field, so you can expect the content to be excellent, content rich and pretty well up to date.

■ They distil the key facts and figures for you, which can save you an inordinate amount of time poring over books, reading journals and creating pages and pages of notes.

Defining idea...

'There are two different kinds of people in this world: those who finish what they start, and'
BRAD RAMSEY

■ They are ideal for your last-minute revision. In fact, my son recently used his study guide in this way before taking a science modular exam. It clearly worked, because he got an A.

Study guides are a great help, but they should not be the be-all and end-all of your studying. As a cautionary tale, a dear friend had bought every study guide possible for each of the subjects he was studying. He would read, re-read and read again each of the guides, believing that these were the panacea to all his studying problems. When it came to the day of his first exam he was able to regurgitate almost word for word the contents of the study guides. Now, one would have expected his results to have been top notch. Well, not quite. The problem was, he had learnt the material so well that he was able to recall the material almost verbatim. This caused a few issues with the examiners, who thought he'd been cheating! Needless to say, it took him quite some time to prove that he had indeed learnt the material and not copied it during the exam. The lesson that I, and my friend, took from all this is that, although study guides are very helpful, you still need to be able to introduce some original thought into your answer, as this is what separates the average student from the truly exceptional. If you want to be exceptional, you're going to have to put in a bit of hard work too.

With a tendency towards course work and projects/ dissertations, basic study guides may not be enough: what you need is to visit IDEA 34, *Dreaming of dissertations*.

Try another idea...

'We are like dwarfs on the shoulders of giants, so that we can see more than they, and things at a greater distance, not by virtue of any sharpness of sight on our part, or any physical distinction, but because we are carried high and raised up by their giant size.'
BERNARD OF CHARTRES

Defining idea...

How did it go?

Q   Just how many study guides should I have?

A   *Guides are best used in those instances where you have a limited grasp of the subject. Having said that, even if your subject knowledge is more extensive, they can still offer some additional input, which is always useful. The beauty is that they set out the key information in an accessible way. They also tend to cover the exams and how to answer specific questions by providing you with model answers.*

Q   Can I rely on the study guide to get me through the exam?

A   *As ever, this depends on your risk appetite and how energetic you feel about studying. I have never relied solely on a study guide because they are really designed to give you just enough to get through the exam, not to excel. In order to excel, you need to answer more than just the question.*

Q   Don't they get out of date?

A   *There is always that problem, but apart from particularly fast-moving fields, most subjects don't change much from year to year, so the basic content will probably stay the same. Also, you should take heart that most publishers will aim to keep their study guides up to date in order to ensure as many students buy them as possible!*

9
Too many cooks?

Ah, the joy of group projects. Love them or hate them, they are there to test your team working skills and to get your creative juices flowing.

Working on a joint project can be exhilarating and exasperating at the same time. To get the best out of them, you need organisational and political skills. They can be fun, honest!

Group projects are more popular than ever because there is a belief that they prepare you for working life, where things like teamwork and cooperation are increasingly important. Now there is a fundamental difference between work and study, and sometimes group projects can be a real pain, especially when *you've* done all the hard work and the others get the mark irrespective of what they have (or have not) done to contribute. Well, that's the way the cookie crumbles, and I should know. When you are assigned a group project it can often involve the use of a video, some very poor acting on your part and a dry subject that needs to be brought alive. These can be a lot of fun if you get it right. And getting it right means – yes you've guessed it – plenty of planning and persistence. I was part of a team of

Here's an idea for you... If you find yourself faced with a group project, get your team together before you start to agree roles and define the principles under which you will all work. This really helps to foster a common understanding of how you are going to work as a team and keeps any friction that occurs during the work to a minimum. Something else to consider is the criteria against which the marks will be divided. This might appear a bit divisive, but the project as a whole depends on people pulling their weight and everyone should be fairly rewarded for their input.

five who had to produce a video during my Masters degree. We decided what the plot would be, scripted it out and then spent hours filming, cutting and editing the final product. It was great fun. And at the end of it, we even showed the outtakes, which some thought was the best part of it. So if you are given a group project, think about the following:

■ What is it that you are going to do? This might sound like a stupid question, but it is vital to make sure you define your tasks carefully, as otherwise you could all end up wasting your time.

■ Appoint a project manager. Like anything in life which involves more than one person, a leader has to be in place to make it happen.

■ Who is going to do what? Everyone needs to have a role if you are to share the final mark fairly.

In order to get the most out of a group project it is helpful to know how a bunch of people become productive. Any group will pass through five stages, and knowing this can help you get to grips with the team as well as the task in hand. The five stages are:

1. Forming – this is where you all come together for the first time and you may not know everyone. So this stage is all about getting to know one another.

2. Storming – this is the messy bit! Having got to know each other, everyone begins to jockey for power and conflict between the group members emerges as each person begins to find their place in the team. Although uncomfortable, this is an essential part of the team development process and is central to becoming high performing.

3. Norming – here things calm down a lot, and this is where the team identity and roles become accepted. This is also where people begin to feel that the purpose of the team is greater than the role of its members and is why having a clear objective helps. You also find that individual members begin to like and support each other.

4. Performing – the fun bit, where the team does great stuff, gets the job done and has a great time.

5. Adjourning – where everyone goes back to normal. Now assuming that the process has been fun, most of the team members won't want to break up and can feel quite sad at the prospect.

If you want to exploit the team spirit you have established in your group project (or projects), get your group involved with communal revision exercises nearer the exams. IDEA 22, *Many hands make light work*, will show you how.

Try another idea…

'*Do not quench your inspiration and your imagination; do not become the slave of your model.*'
VINCENT VAN GOGH

Defining idea…

39

How did it go?

Q   Can I choose my project team?

A   *Sometimes it is possible to select you own team, but from my experience teams are often allocated randomly, which makes the whole process that bit harder. Of course, given the choice, we would all like to select our own teams. Brings back vivid memories from the playground...and why was I always the last one waiting to be picked exactly?*

Q   How do I cope with the infighting?

A   *I find the best way to avoid infighting and power struggles is to appoint a leader as soon as the group comes together for the first time. If you all agree on the leader, then at least there's an arbiter to resolve any disputes.*

Q   What if I have done more than my fair share of the work?

A   *This is always a tricky one to deal with. I think the first thing to do is to have a round-table discussion with your group to see if everyone has contributed the same. If they haven't, you might be able to allocate marks differently. If this fails, you could always raise the matter with your tutor, though my experience suggests that tutors aren't that bothered or keen to get involved. If there is still inequity, at least you can be smug in the knowledge that it's not you who is the freeloader.*

10

Too much information

How on earth do you manage all the information, facts, figures, case studies and examples you're expected to remember? Where do you start?

At times I suspect you've sat at your desk with a pile of books, papers and journals wondering how you'll read them all. To get through this stage of the study cycle and not just give up, you must beat the bumph.

The first step to cutting through the bumph is to understand the difference between bumph and information. Bumph is all the information you may collect during your study, which could include conversations with tutors, group study sessions, books, lecture notes, ideas from the internet and so on. All this stuff finds its way into your brain, which then attempts to categorise and make sense of it all. Information, however, is the stuff which is informative and useful for you in your studies. So the idea behind this entry is to minimise the bumph and maximise the information. But how to do it? There are a number of ways, including:

- Improving your information handling and absorption abilities by making your reading more effective. The way to do this is to set yourself a goal, question or

Here's an idea for you... **We all have the ability to speed read, so give it a go. Take a book which you intend to use for your study. Rather than reading each word in turn, try and pick out blocks of words using your peripheral vision. Your brain is capable of pattern recognition, so go with it. Now go through the chapter again, but this time running your index finger in an 'S' shape from the top to the bottom of each page. As you do so, follow your finger down the page and avoid looking for individual words. Keep practising and you should be able to speed up your reading in no time. If you apply all of the above, you will be well on the way to having an information packed and hence highly productive study. Well done!**

objective before you start reading. This has two benefits. The first is that it gets your subconscious mind working on answering the question in hand, which in turn will help it to filter out irrelevant material and connect everything that is relevant together. And secondly, it helps you to reduce the amount of material you need to read because you will be able to make a quick pass to eliminate those paragraphs which have little or no benefit. For example, an objective like 'I need to understand the basics of post-glacial landforms' will allow you to focus only on the information that supports the goal. And rather than read hundreds of pages, you can scan them for the facts that you need right now. At the same time, it will help your subconscious mind categorise and connect the pieces together.

■ Prioritising your reading so that you spend the right amount of time on the right sources rather than trying to read everything. To do this requires two things: first, you will need to be more critical of what you are reading; and secondly, you should recognise what information you really need. So for the former you will have to be prepared to dismiss things which are unlikely to add value to your study, and for the second you will need to figure out what you will use the newly acquired information for.

Now you've beaten the bumph and can read effectively, put your information to good use by building a few model answers à la IDEA 26, *Blueprint for success*.

Try another idea...

- Knowing when to ditch the useless stuff. We can accumulate vast amounts of information in the form of books, articles and printouts from the Net. And how often do we make photocopies and collect stuff with the 'I think this might come in useful' in mind and then never use it? I used to have box files crammed full of cuttings which I thought would come in handy. Only a small percentage of them ever did. So the advice here is that if you are not going to use it immediately, you probably won't use it at all.

- Improve your reading habits. There are two elements to this one too. The first is to read faster and the second is to enhance your comprehension. There are many ways to improve your reading speed and there are plenty of courses available to teach you them. In some cases you can end up so that the action of merely popping your index figure on a page will allow you to absorb all the information in one go. Comprehension is another matter. Our ability to retain the information we have read attenuates rapidly: within about 20 minutes we are only able to remember around 20 per cent of what we've read unless we use it. So the

'Let thy words be few.'
ECCLESIASTES 5:2

Defining idea...

key here is to do some or all of the following: read critically (i.e. with a goal in mind); don't reread what you have already covered as it will already be in your head, it's just that you haven't recognised it yet; and take regular breaks.

How did
it go?

Q   I'm worried I might miss something, so should I read every word?

A   *No. You are far better off capturing those things which are most important. Having a goal really helps to avoid this problem. You should also remember that most books and articles have been padded out to fill the space. Look for that golden nugget.*

Q   How can I set myself realistic targets?

A   *The best way is to use past papers, or the syllabus if you have one to hand, and use these to pick out some objectives against which you can read.*

Q   I collect lots of cuttings and articles just in case they are useful. What should I do?

A   *Articles and cuttings can of course be invaluable sources of information for your study. The problem is that they soon accumulate, and before long you end up with even more material to get through! So the way to approach it is as follows. As you tear the article out, ask yourself the following two questions: (1) for what purpose am I going to use this? (2) Can I use it right now? If you can't answer the first question and answer to the second is no, then throw it away as you may never get round to it.*

11

Fewer snakes, more ladders

If studying and exams were a game of snakes and ladders, wouldn't you want to have more ladders than snakes? In the world of study, 'exam briefings' are there to be climbed whereas bunking off can only bring you down.

Most institutions, be they schools, universities or cookery clubs, want as many of their students to pass as possible. In fact, they'll hold 'exam briefings' to give as many hints and tips to their students as possible. Shouldn't you attend?

One of the simplest errors students of any kind can make is to fail to attend an exam briefing session. Such sessions are invaluable because they help you to get to grips with the trials ahead, namely the dreaded exams. Most are run a few weeks before the exams start so that everyone has the opportunity to complete their revision in time, even those of us who leave most of it to the last minute.

Here's an idea for you... **The next time an exam review session is announced for your class, make sure you attend. When you are there listen attentively and take as many notes as possible. These events are golden opportunities for you to improve your chances of being successful in your exams – and gold is the colour of success.**

Their format varies according to the type of exam and type of institution. Within schools they are mainly focused on giving you hints and tips on how to perform to your best in the actual exams. They will also provide guidance on the syllabus and how best to answer certain types of question. That's all the school is able to do, because the questions are set by an external examination board. Within those institutions that also control the setting of the exams, such as universities, you can get much more, as here it is the examiners themselves (who also happen to be your tutors/lecturers) who give you the advice. As such, the information they give can cover all sorts of useful things, like which topics you should focus on and how the exams are marked. I have never been disappointed. I attended some of the best exam briefings whilst studying for my Masters degree. There I was told how the exams were going to be marked, how best to manage my time during the exams, which topics were worth studying and, in some cases, what kind of question might come up (which was particularly helpful). They also hinted at which subjects might be worth leaving off the revision list, which was just as useful. This made all the difference to my subsequent revision because it gave me a real confidence boost.

So, having attended one of these sessions, what should you do with all that invaluable information? I recommend the following:

Thanks for buying one of our books! If you'd like to be placed on our mailing list to receive more information on forthcoming releases in the **52 Brilliant Ideas** series just send an e-mail to *info@infideas.com* with your name and address or simply fill in the details below and pop this card in the post. No postage is needed. We promise we won't do silly things like bombard you with lots of junk mail, nor would we even consider letting third parties look at your details. Ever.

Name:..

Address:..

....

e-mail:..

Which book did you purchase?..

....

Tell us what you thought of this book and our series; check out the 'Brilliant Communication' bit on the other side of this card.

I am interested in the following subjects:

☐ Health & relationships
☐ Lifestyle & leisure
☐ Arts, literature and music

☐ Careers, finance & personal development
☐ Sports, hobbies & games
☐ Actually, I'd be quite interested in:..

And just to say thanks, every month we'll pick 3 random names from a hat (ok, it may be some other cylindrical device) and send a complimentary book from the series. It could be you. So please tell us what book you'd like:..(check out www.52brilliantideas.com for a full list of our titles, or if you prefer we can choose one for you based on your subject interest).

You can change your life with brilliant ideas.

We're passionate about the effect our books have and we have designed them so that they can become an inspiring part of your daily routine. Our books help people to grow, giving them the confidence to believe in themselves and to transform their lives. Every day, around the world, people are regaining control of their lives with our brilliant ideas.

infiniteideas

www.52brilliantideas.com

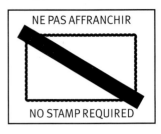
Brilliant Communication

- If you enjoyed this book and find yourself cuddling it at night, please tell us. If you think this book isn't fit to use as kindling, please let us know. We value your thoughts and need your honest feedback. We know if we listen to you we'll get it right. Why not send us an e-mail at *listeners@infideas.com*.

- Do you have a brilliant idea of your own that our author has missed? E-mail us at *yourauthor missedatrick@infideas.com* and if it makes it into print in a future edition or appears on our web site we'll send you four books of your choice OR the cash equivalent. You'll be fully credited (if you want) so that everyone knows you've had a brilliant idea.

- Finally, if you've enjoyed one of our books why not become an **Infinite Ideas Ambassador**. Simply e-mail ten of your friends enlightening them about the virtues of the **52 Brilliant Ideas** series and dishing out our web address: www.52brilliantideas.com. Make sure you copy us in at *ambassador@infideas.com*. We promise we won't contact them unless they contact us, but we'll send you a free book of your choice for every ten friends you email. Help spread the word!

- First, compare what you have just heard to your existing plan of action. And if you didn't have a plan, now you should be armed with everything you need to create one. If there is anything that you haven't already covered or something that you now feel requires a little more work, adjust your revision timetable to take account of it.

To get the best out of your studying it is important to know when you are at your most productive. Tune in to IDEA 17, *Morning, noon and night*, for some useful pointers.

Try another idea...

- If you have been given some broad tips on what some, or perhaps all, of the questions might be, it's a good idea to consider narrowing your revision a bit so that you can spend more time on those subjects. It will also be worthwhile reading around the selected topics for background information, and checking a few past papers to get a gist of what the examiners are looking for.

- Finally, take some time to review how your current revision approach will allow you to maximise your marks whilst minimising your workload. It's a case of working smarter, not harder. The tips you will get about marking, for example, should guide you towards better time management. This is a good opportunity to review how well your approach to studying and revising is working. At this stage in the process, you still have plenty of time to take on board other ideas and techniques.

'Get the advice of everybody whose advice is worth having – they are very few – and then do what you think best yourself.'
CHARLES STEWART PARNELL

Defining idea...

Q **I feel I'm already on top of everything, so why should I attend?**

A   *No matter how well prepared you think you are, these sessions are still well worth attending. The additional information they provide will either reinforce your level of preparedness, thereby giving a boost to your confidence, or identify gaps in your approach.*

Q **How much of the advice should I follow?**

A   *The more general advice should always be followed because it is plain common sense. The more specific advice should be taken as guidance. Because such briefings can't give you everything, I would always keep one or two topics up your sleeve to hedge your bets. It's always dangerous to put all of your faith in what you've heard, so I wouldn't recommend that.*

Q **What if my education centre doesn't offer a revision session?**

A   *If you find yourself without this kind of support, there is no harm in seeking some individual input from your tutor or teacher. They ought to be able to give you some hints and tips. And if there is no formal session organised, why not see if you can get one jacked up? Not only will you benefit, but your fellow students will as well.*

12

Tick, tock

Managing time is a skill which every student has to master. From developing a study timetable to making sure you spend your time effectively in the exam hall, every second counts.

It's ironic, isn't it? We talk about time management and yet we are no more capable of truly managing time than we are of holding back the tides.

But even King Canute would have had better results if he had prioritised his time properly and had lunch before tackling the waves.

I wonder how many people can actually say with confidence that they are expert at managing their time? I would guess very few. When it comes to studying, and especially revision, I'm sure this number drops considerably, especially as it is a repetitive and dull process. The great news is that if you can get good at using time productively then you can reduce the number of hours you have to spend poring over books, notes and papers. So what do the masters of time management suggest? First, you have to know what saps your time. The key time wasters associated with studying are:

- Interruptions of any kind.

Here's an idea for you... **Make a list of all your exam dates as soon as they become available. Once you are armed with this information, work backwards a few weeks until you believe you have arrived at a date when you intend to start you revision. Now set yourself weekly and then daily targets of what you are expecting to have achieved. And, as you get nearer the exams themselves, prioritise where to focus your efforts.**

■ Crisis management, or in other words, leaving everything to the last minute (yes, crammers, it's you I'm talking about).

■ Unclear objectives and priorities.

■ Having no plan.

■ Stress and tiredness.

■ Personal organisation (I'm afraid you will have to tidy your desk and room, as otherwise how are you going to find your notes when you need them?).

If any of these affect you, it's time you got clockwise and understood the value of time management.

In order to make sure you get the best use out of the time available, I recommend that you:

■ Tackle the most difficult areas of study and revision first. Sure, it's easy to procrastinate and do the easy stuff before anything else, but you are better off focusing on the tough material first as the longer you leave it, the more difficult it gets to face up to. Then you'll never get around to it, you'll get stressed out and things will go on a downward spiral.

■ Prioritise your time. Don't try and do all your revision in one go: assess what needs to be done and then determine what order you are going to tackle it in.

- Avoid any form of distraction. Unplug the internet and turn off your precious mobile phone.

- If you are going to work with others make sure you set yourselves objectives. Otherwise you may well have a great time, but you'll achieve nothing.

Once you get to grips with the whole time management thing and feel on top of the syllabus, check out IDEA 14, *One step beyond*, for the benefits of reading around your subject.

Try another idea...

- If you are studying alongside a day job and family, make sure you allocate your time carefully. Your spouse and children do want to see you, you know.

- Make a plan. As the Royal Engineers taught me, planning and preparation prevents p*** poor performance. If you stick to your plan you will be just fine.

Analysing how you spend your time during your study periods by jotting down what you do over the course of a week or so can help too. You'll be surprised at just how unfocused you are. I know I was before I recognised the value of time management.

Time management also comes into the exam itself and, if anything, is far more important then. Not having completed the paper before you hear those immortal words 'Put your pens down' is a heart-stopping experience, often closely preceded by the blind panic of trying to complete the final question in less than 30 seconds. (Yes, I've been there, done that and learnt the lesson.) So to avoid that seizure moment, make sure you know exactly how much time you have got for each question and stick to it. You may not completely finish every question, but you will get more marks than if you only completed two out of three.

'The future depends on what we do in the present.'
MAHATMA GANDHI

Defining idea...

How did it go?

Q How detailed should my study timetable be?

A This depends on how far away you are from the exams. If you are months away, I would allocate a day per subject. As you get to within, say, 2–3 weeks of the exams, I would go to half-day or quarter-day slots. Then within a week I would shorten them further, perhaps even hourly. This will begin to get you used to working under pressure, which should also help you in the exams themselves.

Q Can I take an alarm clock into the exam?

A Although the exam hall will have a clock which should be visible to all the students, there are advantages of having some kind of clock or even stopwatch on your desk. First, it keeps you focused on your desk and not on what's going on around the room. Secondly, if you have a stopwatch and set it to the time allotted for each question, you can make sure you don't spend any more time on them than you should. A word of advice, though: don't set the alarm!

Q What if I'm hopeless at time management (OK, I admit it – I am)?

A You could try getting a book on the subject, or even attending a course if you really feel the need. Most people who are poor at time management are only like that because they can't prioritise. So my advice is to get a pen and paper right now and start by making a list. You'll soon get the hang of it.

13

Spotting the winners

If you're struggling with the amount of revision you've got to do, why not try something completely different? It's time to cut to the chase and get your binoculars out. Yes, it's time to go question spotting.

Focusing on a few key topics might seem like a high-risk strategy, but what better way to concentrate your revision? Study them well and you'll be successful. The art, of course, is figuring out which ones to study.

So you've been sweating hard poring over the syllabus and thinking to yourself, 'How on earth am I going to learn all this stuff?' Well the simple answer is, you don't have to. No, I'm not suggesting that you throw in the towel just yet, but I am offering up a way of limiting the volume of work you need to do to prepare for your exams. In the early period of my exam-taking career I used to try and learn everything in the syllabus. The piles of books, papers and notes would cover my desk and at times I would feel overwhelmed with the amount of stuff I had to get through. In hindsight, I'm not sure how productive or, indeed, successful this was.

Knowing what areas of the syllabus to focus on is about targeting your revision to what past exam papers are telling you about this year's papers. So get hold of, say, three to five years' worth of exam papers and look at them carefully. Before long you'll start to see some patterns emerging. Similar questions will pop up every few years: they might be worded slightly differently, but the basic idea behind them will be the same. Once you've identified the pattern, you can work out what questions might come up when you sit your exams. And hey presto, a lot of your workload has vanished!

Then one of my friends introduced me to question spotting, which he had been using to great effect. Question spotting is an exam and study technique that is incredibly simple: all it entails is working out what questions might appear on your exam paper and then only revising those topics. It didn't take me long to see some of the immediate advantages…focused revision and an opportunity to augment my answers with information from other sources. As soon as I embraced it I felt liberated – and you can too.

Question spotting is part art and part science. The art comes from the application of judgement and the willingness to take a few risks when it comes to focusing your study. The science – well, pseudo-science really – comes from deducing the best topic areas to focus on. If the idea of question spotting appeals to you, then it's best to start on a subject that you feel most comfortable with and attempt a dry run. I find this helps to build confidence in your ability to use the technique. Another approach to help you hone your question-spotting skills is to use past papers from subjects that you are not studying: after all, patterns are patterns, and you can develop your expertise without worrying about messing up.

Once you are confident, you can begin to apply the approach to the subjects you are studying. You can always test your question-spotting skills by holding one past paper back and trying to predict the questions on it from what you have just learnt. Another dead cert for the question spotter is when the syllabus changes. You can almost guarantee that the examiners will set a question on the new topics they introduce – otherwise, why would they bother introducing them in the first place? Plus most students would feel cheated (well, I would) if they had to study a new theme without ever being tested on it.

If missing chunks out of the syllabus out of your study makes you nervous, why not attend one of the revision sessions run by your tutors? IDEA 11, *Fewer snakes, more ladders*, should get you moving in the right direction.

Try another idea...

As I mentioned earlier, one of the advantages to question spotting is that it buys you more time. You can choose to spend this as you please (but wisely, of course!). For me, it affords the chance to build up knowledge of my favourite subjects beyond that which has been covered in the formal teaching environment by background reading. If anything, this means that you are studying for more than just the exam, and you will undoubtedly learn more. You are also likely to pick up more marks.

'It is amazing how quickly the kids learn to drive a car, yet are unable to understand the lawnmower, snowblower or vacuum cleaner.'
BEN BERGOR, vaudevillian magician

Defining idea...

How did
it go?

Q **I feel very uneasy about reducing my study to a small number of areas. Should I still give it a go?**

A   *It's quite natural to feel the need to cover as much of the syllabus as possible; in fact, you'll have been conditioned to do just that by your tutors. In the end, it's a matter of choice and confidence. If you want to learn every element of the syllabus, that's fine. But I believe the only thing holding you back from question spotting is a bit of practice.*

Q **How many topics should I focus on?**

A   *This is driven by two things: first, the number of questions you will be expected to answer in the exam; and secondly, how confident you feel that you have spotted them correctly. The former is easy to find out, but the latter depends on the level of risk you are comfortable with. I tend to go for the minimum plus one or perhaps two back-up topics. So if you have to answer three questions out of ten, I would spot five.*

Q **Could I screw things up in the exam if the questions don't come up as planned?**

A   *The simple answer to this is yes, you could, and I have been caught out on the odd occasion. But we should be realistic about this because it is usually only one question that might not appear, not all of them. This is why it is helpful to have a couple of other topics up your sleeve, because it reduces the instant panic you'll have when you realise not all the topics you have spotted have come up.*

14

One step beyond

Once you've covered the whole syllabus, you should have done everything you need to be successful, right? Well, yes and no. Certainly, you ought to pass, but to pass well will require a little bit more.

Whilst preparing for my exam, my geography tutor suggested I read a couple of extra books. They helped me get brilliant marks because they showed the examiners that I had mastered the subject, not just the syllabus.

Exam results usually adhere to a normal distribution, which means that not everyone will get the highest grades. So if you want to achieve the highest grade, you're going to need to do more than just the basics; you will have to read around the subject. This means picking up additional ideas and concepts which you can add to your study, revision and, most importantly, exam answers. Now it would be a complete waste of time to make this untargeted – let's be honest, outlining the philosophy behind Shaker furniture is not going to help you expound on the finer intricacies of the cheese-making process – so the best way to focus your

Jot down the syllabus and what you know about it, like key thinkers, major theories and primary examples. Then pop down to your library and look for books associated with the subject. As you flick through them, look for additional ideas, concepts and examples which you could use. Make brief notes about any you find and add them to your syllabus outline. If you do this early on in your study, you can concentrate on your core subject nearer the exams.

extracurricular activity is to make sure that the additional material you pick up is directly related to the syllabus. And in order to keep this new material to a manageable level, it's a good idea to answer the following questions:

- What other examples could help to illustrate a particular point of view or component of the syllabus?

- Who are the latest and most up-to-date thinkers on the subject, and what is their perspective?

- What are the latest theories or ideas about the subject?

In answering each of these questions you should be able to generate some really solid examples and additional viewpoints that you can weave into your answer. Examples are especially useful because they help to set your answer aside from the average student's response. When used properly they clearly demonstrate to the examiners that you know more about the subject than most, which will secure additional marks and potentially that elusive A grade. Capturing information on the latest thinkers and their theories is also a great way to pick up more marks because it shows that you have extended your understanding of the subject – in essence, that you have mastered it – and it is this that separates an A-grade student from the rest. It is important to remember that academics are now expected to publish their research more frequently than in the past, so there should always be plenty of new stuff around for you to draw on.

I always remember reading a couple of books about primary cities for human geography. The examples I distilled from them and the theories as to why primary cities existed helped me enormously in the exam I sat. As I was trying to figure out which question I could answer next, not one but two jumped out at me. Although both were different, I was able to use the same examples to illustrate the points I needed to make. Now if that's not payback, I don't know what is.

To get the full benefit of reading beyond the subject, explore the technique of mind mapping, as laid out in IDEA 16, Let me look into your mind.

Try another idea...

'*The secret to creativity is knowing how to hide your sources.*'
ALBERT EINSTEIN

Defining idea...

How did it go?

Q **I feel overloaded enough without having to study even more. Why should I bother?**

A *Sure, it may seem daunting to add additional material to your already huge pile, but the benefits to be had are very real. If you adopt one of the numerous summarising techniques available, this increase may not seem too onerous after all.*

Q **Can you apply this idea to all subjects?**

A *The approach generally applies to subjects which require an essay-based answer in the exam. Because of this, it tends to be more applicable to the humanities than the sciences. It is also useful to apply this approach to coursework, as you will pick up additional marks without the stress of the exam.*

Q **Where can I find the additional information I need?**

A *There are plenty of sources. Books are an obvious place to start, but I find that journals are even better as these are where you will find the latest thinking and examples. Most subjects have journals associated with them (sometimes hundreds!), where academics publish their latest research. Your library should have some, if not all, in stock, and if they don't hold them, they should be more than happy to order copies for you. Another source of information is the internet, which, assuming you have the patience to cut through the mountains of hits, can be very useful too.*

15

Life, the universe and everything...but what's the question?

Struggling with what those exam questions are really looking for is one of the perennial problems of the student. But how to sort the inquisitorial wheat from the questionable chaff?

The thing that used to catch me out in exams was the flowery words used to frame the questions. Some examination boards are worse than others for this. I even changed exam boards once to pass a maths exam because I couldn't understand the questions!

Let's face it, the worst time to be interpreting the examiner's question is during the exam. You are probably feeling a tad nervous and worried about how little time you have to answer the questions. Adding the problem of figuring out what the examiner wants is only going to compound your woes. So, the best way to avoid this additional

Get hold of some past exam papers and create outline answers for each type of question. So for a compare and contrast type question, draw up an outline and then check it against a model answer, if one exists. After a while you'll get used to, and hence tuned into, the types of question you will face in the exam.

panic is to work out what the wording means...long before the exam. If you have sussed out the hidden question behind the key words, then you're going to find the exam much easier.

Here are the commonly used words which crop up time and time again in exams and, more importantly, here is what they mean:

Compare and contrast. Very common indeed and can be used either singularly (as in compare existentialism with Buddhism) or together. Whenever a question asks you to compare two things, it is inviting you to identify the similarities between them. Conversely, and not unexpectedly, when you are asked to contrast two things, the examiner is looking for the differences between them. This is why, when used together, compare and contrast is a great way to test your reasoning and logic skills.

Categorise. This is straightforward in so far as the examiner is asking you to organise the components of a topic in a logical way, which might require you to create a table, list or taxonomy. However, although this might not be explicit in the question (and indeed, what question ever is explicit?), the examiner is also seeking some reasoning for the categorisation you have chosen to use. So, when asked to categorise the religions of the world, for example, you would be expected to both list or tabulate the religions and describe the basis for the structure you have used.

'Never say more than is necessary.'
RICHARD BRINSLEY SHERIDAN

Analyse, evaluate or critique. This is asking you to identify the pros and cons of a particular subject, such as the presidency of George Bush. So here you will need to come up with the positive things and negative things about the subject. You will also be expected to arrive at some kind of conclusion, so don't get too carried away! Sometimes examiners will ask you to justify an argument or line of reasoning which will require you to focus on one line of argument only.

If you're hard wired to associate exams and study with pain but want to be better at studying and more confident in your exams, IDEA 31, *No gain without pain*, will show you how to go about rewiring.

Try another idea...

Discuss. Probably one of the hardest questions to deal with because it is expecting a wide-ranging review of the topic and it's easy to get seduced into dumping everything you know about the subject onto paper. The art is to provide as much information as possible without writing *War and Peace* and losing precious time.

Illustrate. This question is all about providing examples and how they can be used to support a particular argument or statement posed by the question. So 'Illustrate how the cold war was waged between the Soviet Union and the West' could involve providing examples like the Berlin Blockade, the building of the Berlin Wall, Korea and Vietnam and so on.

Summarise. This type of question is asking you to be concise and relatively brief. What it is looking for will to some extent depend on the context of the question, as it might be looking for a list ('Summarise the changes that are brought about by glaciers') or a more detailed discussion ('Summarise the debate surrounding the US government's war on drugs').

So there you have it, a summary of the common types of question you should expect to see cropping up on any exam paper.

Q I can't get to grips with this whole question thing. Will I always be this confused?

A *To be fair, it does take a long time to get to grips with this. The unfortunate thing is that every examining board and university adopts a slightly different style. Some are more direct than others. The best thing to do is to keep at it and use past papers to practise with.*

Q Should I aim to focus on becoming expert at one or two variants?

A *This may not be a bad idea, especially if the examining board favours particular questions, like compare and contrast. The key, as ever, is to reach a level of confidence that allows you to cope with the curved ball in the exam. The art here is to ensure that you are at your best in the exam and capable of creating a superb answer.*

Q How can I remember the myriad of questions?

A *I find the best way is to create a cue card which defines each type of question, what it means and the types of things you need to do when answering them. If you lay it out as a simple table you should be able to use it to develop an automatic response when you see the question. Once you've got it cracked, in the exam you'll be able to focus on the content of the answer rather than the question.*

16

Let me look into your mind

One of the hardest jobs when it comes to studying is distilling your copious notes into a manageable number of words, pictures, key words and bullet points that you can remember. One of the best methods is mind mapping.

I was never one for distillation — not of my notes, anyway. All my attempts resulted in a similar volume to what I had before. After too many years of reading and re-reading vast piles of paper I learnt the art of mind mapping. Eureka! No more lever arch files: all I needed were a few mind maps and everything came flooding back.

The mind is an extremely powerful thing – more powerful than you'd probably imagine. It has seemingly infinite capacity, which permits us to learn as much (or as little) as we'd like, and what's so great about it is that, unlike our bodies, we can't overfeed it! So, what does this mean for studying? Quite simply, that with the appropriate tools, techniques and training we can absorb all those notes we've made and, more importantly, remember them all. Enter the mind map, which was devised

Grab a piece of paper and draw a cloud in the centre of the page. Take one of your subjects (let's take physical geography as an example). Write Physical Geography in the cloud and then draw lines from the cloud. Each line should represent a branch of the subject, like rivers, weather and so on. Draw further lines from these words to provide further categorisation. So with rivers you might have confluence, oxbow lakes, rejuvenation and so on. Carry on until you have completed your mind map.

by the now-famous Tony Buzan. The mind-mapping technique works on the principle of engaging both the right and left hemispheres of your brain. In so doing, it mimics the way the brain packages, retains and recalls information. For those of you who don't know what each hemisphere does, here's a potted lesson. The left side looks after the logical stuff, like words, numbers and analysis, while the right side looks after the imaginative stuff, including pictures, spatial positioning, colours and the like. Now that's sorted, here's how to create a mind map.

Sit down with a blank piece of paper and pick a subject which you are studying. Once you've decided on the subject, pick out a key topic. For example, if it's history you are studying, you might choose the Wars of the Roses. Write this at the centre of the page and enclose it in a box, bubble or cloud. Now consider the topic, and for each line of thought draw a line radiating out from the central box (or bubble or cloud). The thickness of the line should represent the importance of that line of thought. So you may have a thick line with key battles written along it, or key personalities. Then you can draw thinner lines from the end of the thick lines to highlight the next level of distillation. So for the battles you would have lines for the battles of Towton, Tewkesbury, Bosworth and Barnet and so on. If you want to add further facts about the battles, you draw even thinner lines from each and annotate them with the information you need to recall – like the number of dead and wounded, for example. The process may seem almost endless, but you will eventually run out of things to capture. If you are really sophisticated, you can draw the odd picture to act as an additional memory jogger.

By completing the mind map you will have achieved two things. First, you will have reinforced your prior learning through the creation of the mind map. Secondly, you will have developed a neat summary of the topic you need to revise. Coincidentally, the final product – the mind map – resembles the brain in outline, as the one I have included for exam techniques shows.

If you're not entirely convinced by mind maps, try condensing your notes onto cue cards, as encapsulated in IDEA 18, *The word that launched a thousand notes*.

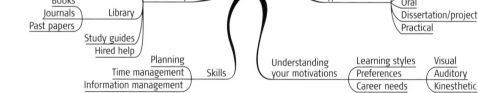

There are distinct advantages to be gained from using mind maps. First, they play into the way your mind works, which means that recalling information should be generally easier. They also allow you to make linkages between key strands of information more readily. In addition, they allow you to add new information

Defining idea...

'One must learn by doing the thing; for though you think you know it you have no certainty, until you try.'
SOPHOCLES

without having to rewrite everything, which is often the case with written notes, and finally they are simpler to recall. So give it a go, get tuned into the natural way your brain works and develop total recall.

How did it go?

Q   I have looked at a mind map and it looks terribly fancy. Do I have to make mine look the same?

A   *Not at all. In fact, mine are all very simple. I start with a bubble in the middle of my page and use lines and words only. In the end, it is all about making the concept work for you. So don't worry about the style of your mind map – a warped map does not indicate a warped mind – it is the general principle and content that count.*

Q   Is there any software out there that supports mind mapping?

A   *Yes. Some of it you have to purchase, but other programs are freeware. The beauty of software is that you don't have to write it yourself and it supports the more sophisticated maps you need to draw.*

Q   How detailed should the mind maps be?

A   *This is very much down to you and the amount of information you feel comfortable about displaying. The beauty of mind maps is that there are no finite limits, so you can make them as big and as detailed as you like. I prefer to work on the basis of filling a single page of A4; this way, I can keep my key subjects to a manageable size.*

17

Morning, noon and night

When do you feel most productive? Do you deliver the goods when the milkman is delivering his, or do you tuck in when most sane people are tucked up in bed? Whatever your natural preference, that's the time to study.

I have never been a great fan of mornings, but I always felt compelled to drag myself out of my bed and get some studying done. I may have felt sanctimonious, but sitting there doodling and dreaming of bed was not very productive.

Now, of course, I know better, thanks to all those boffins who have looked into our sleeping patterns.

It is now known that there are two types of people: morning types (also known as larks) and evening types (also known as owls). Admittedly there are also those who think larking around is a hoot no matter what the time of day, but they're probably

Here's an idea for you...

Find out your peak period the following way. Over the course of a week study at specific times and assess your levels of alertness and effectiveness. So on Monday, you might get up at 06:00 and study until 10:00 am. On Tuesday you could get up at 09:00 and study between 12:00 and 16:00. On another day you could have a longer lie in, busy yourself during the day then get down to study at 19:00 and work through until 23:00. When recording your levels of alertness and effectiveness, note how awake you feel, how focused you are and how productive you are. It shouldn't be long before you have sussed out your prime time. If you forget to record one day, don't worry – it's probably a sign that the day's regime was definitely not working for you!

not the studying type so we won't concern ourselves with them here. As you'd expect, the larks amongst us love getting up at the crack of dawn, feel full of energy and rarely go to bed beyond nine in the evening. The opposite is true with the owls. Apparently, our ability to concentrate at the two ends of the day is determined by our genes, and there is little we can do about it. In fact, research has shown that if we ignore our natural body clocks we can do ourselves more harm than good. So it's time (no pun intended) to get to grips with your body clock and study when you're at your peak. I'm not suggesting that it is okay not to turn up for lectures, seminars and tutorials just because your body clock isn't aligned to them. What I am suggesting is that you should match your study regime (the one that you control) to your own body clock.

Another thing that is worth bearing in mind is what is known as sleep debt. Think back to medieval times, before electricity had been understood and tamed, and when the price of oil for lamps was even more than it is today. Sleep cycles would have been determined by the rising and setting of the sun, so people would have expected to sleep for a lot longer than we do today – in the winter at least; summertime would have been party time! In the modern environment, with the almost incessant use of artificial light, we still need to get an average of eight hours of sleep a night. If you are getting less than this, then over the course of a week or so you will build up a sleep debt. If you don't make this deficit back up by having a lie in, you will become more and more tired, and your efficiency and eventually health will start to suffer. This suggests that there is little value in slogging yourself to death by studying all hours. The watchword here is listen to what your body is telling you.

Understanding sleep patterns is a great start to getting the most out of your study, but getting to grips with your study environment is also important. So if it's total silence or loud music, see IDEA 4, *Protect your environment*.

Try another idea...

If the idea of doing what comes naturally appeals, you might want to pick up a book on biorhythms. This will allow you to explore in a lot more detail how natural cycles in the body impact how you feel. You might even choose to link your revision timetable to your biorhythms, but I leave that entirely up to you!

'*Every man has his own destiny; the only imperative is to follow it; to accept it, no matter where it leads him.*'
HENRY MILLER

Defining idea...

How did
it go?

Q How can I judge when to stop studying? I feel guilty if I'm not hard at it all the time, even when I'm tired.

A *I know what you mean. I used to stay up all hours thinking that I had to cram as much study in as possible into my every waking moment. Of course, this was crazy, as I ended up getting more and more tired and less and less productive. So here's some advice: ditch the guilt and tune in to your body clock.*

Q When should I stop, then?

A *You will stop naturally, as once you get tired your brain will begin to wander onto different things and your concentration will fade. Over time, you should become sensitive to the warning signs of study fatigue, and as a result know when you are flogging a dead horse. If you need to sleep, sleep.*

Q Should I set my alarm clock?

A *This depends on when your productive time is. If it happens to be early in the morning, then why not, especially if the peace and quiet at that time of day allows you to concentrate. Your partner may not think its such a good idea, though, if you find yourself constantly setting the alarm for 3 a.m.*

18

The word that launched a thousand notes

Your brain's ability to remember information is phenomenal and if you train it well you can use single words or phrases to recall all your notes as though they were right in front of you.

The tail end of your study — revision and exam preparation — is not an exciting prospect. The fun bit of learning new things is over; now it's time to focus on your regurgitation skills. But there are plenty of ways to reduce the pain...eventually.

An excellent method for coping with the vast amounts of information you need to recall is to condense it into a small number of key words and facts which, when read, will prompt all the information to leap effortlessly into your mind. Admittedly, the process of condensing all those facts, figures, examples and diagrams still requires a lot of effort, but it is far better than reading and re-reading

Here's an idea for you... **Once you have distilled all your notes onto a small number of cards, or sheets of paper, convert them into questions and write them onto Post-it notes. These can be great memory joggers if you place them around the home: behind the bathroom door, on your mirror, on the fridge and so on. As you come across them the questions will prompt you to recall the key facts required to answer them. It's a great way to keep those synapses firing.**

your notes, which can get very tiresome. One of the best ways of condensing your notes is as follows. First you have to make sure that your notes are complete, and if there are gaps, then fill these in before moving on (you might find it helpful to check your notes against the syllabus when looking for gaps). The next step is to read through your notes and highlight words, phrases, images and anything else that is important, and especially those that might be useful for the exam. Whilst doing this you might want to have both the syllabus and a few past exam papers to hand to ensure you have identified everything that could be considered key. Once you have highlighted all the vital information, the next step is to group it by topic and write each topic onto a separate sheet of paper. Then read each in turn and highlight the key words, facts, dates, etc. from this newly summarised information. Keep repeating this process until you are left with a small and manageable number of facts, phrases and key words, which you should then transfer to small cards (index cards, available from a post office or office supplies store near you). You should now have a bunch of cards for each subject, topic and sub-topic which you can now use as the basis for your ongoing revision. The beauty of having cards is they are portable, so you can whip them out whenever you have the chance: on the plane, on the train, at a particularly boring family gathering, and so on.

The process you have just gone through may seem a little tortuous, but it is important because the very act of reading, writing, grouping and condensing helps you to memorise the facts. So, when you read the key word you should be able to recall all of the information you started off with. Having condensed all the key words, phrases and dates onto the front of the card, you can always add additional information, such as diagrams, onto the back. In fact, linking some of the key words to diagrams is an excellent way to reinforce your learning, especially if you respond well to visual triggers.

Sitting down and distilling notes can be a real drag. So in order to keep your interest alive, make sure you take some time out for some much deserved rest and recreation – see IDEA 24, *All work and no play.*

Try another idea...

A word of caution: it's a good idea to label your cards by subject and also to number them. I remember a friend of mine at college who was proudly showing everyone the cue cards he'd just produced for his exams. He tripped and they went flying. We all saw the funny side of it until we realised that he hadn't numbered the cards – when he promptly lost his sense of humour, though we still retained ours! We spent hours helping him put them back into the correct order, which I suppose helped a bit with the learning process, but he made sure he always added numbers from then on.

'The fox knows many things – the hedgehog one big one.'
ARCHILOCHUS

Defining idea...

How did
it go? **Q How many key words and facts should I have?**

A   To a large extent this depends on the complexity of the subject that you are
     trying to condense. I find the best way to arrive at the minimum is to
     continually test your ability to recall information from them. If you find that
     you are still missing out chunks of vital information, then you need to
     include additional key words. This for me is the acid test, as it's all about
     recall.

Q Any tips on organising the cards?

A   I tend to favour the use of a Rolodex, which is what salesmen used for
     years to store client information before the advent of computer databases.
     It allows you to organise the cards into discrete blocks and is neat and tidy.
     Another idea I have tried in the past is to create a concertina by taping the
     cards together.

Q Is this any better than any of the other techniques?

A   No, not necessarily. It's just another alternative for you to try, and if it
     works for you, so much the better. I believe it's a great addition to your
     repertoire of studying tools and techniques, though, and if you mix it in
     with some of the others then you'll have a winning formula. I tend to guard
     against a single technique if only because it can get a bit boring.

19

The power of positive thinking

If there is one thing you need in spades when it comes to studying and taking exams, it's positive thinking.

I'm well known for being someone whose glass is half empty. So I could do with reading this entry; but what about you?

Are you someone you who thinks positively or are you more like me, perhaps a little more jaded and cynical? Well, the news is that if you think positively you will generally do better in life and expect to have good experiences. In other words, because you look for the good rather than the bad in situations, you will find it. But it's more than that; it's about being able to see the opportunities and getting the best out of any situation, no matter how bad. When our attitude is positive we tend to feel better and are more constructive; we are also more effective at deciding what we want to happen, and feel in control. And the brain actually functions better when we are feeling positive, and our general health and body language improve too. Sounds too good to be true.

Here's an idea for you...

The next time you catch yourself getting down about your study, use this simple model, event + response = outcome, to change your response so that the outcome is positive. So instead of thinking 'I'm never going to complete my study' and therefore feeling low about it all, try a different response, like 'I am looking forward to completing my studies so that I can get some free time', which will make you feel better. After a while you will begin to see the positive side to study and this should help keep the blues away.

So how do we get a positive outlook? For starters, we need to learn how to deal with setbacks. Positive thinkers will not beat themselves up about them or believe that they have failed. Instead, they'll learn something from the experience, put it behind them and move on. Another thing to do is avoid the usual fear and loathing that encompasses us (well, in our heads anyway). Typical fears we have include failure, disappointment, unworthiness and even fear of fear itself. The problem with fear is that it holds us back. Positive thinkers recognise fear for what it is – a feeling, and often an irrational one. They don't react to it or defend it. Instead they embrace it and carry on. Heavy stuff this, but a positive outlook allows you to conquer your fears.

Probably the most important thing positive people do is like themselves. They know their own worth and look forward to the future, even though it may be uncertain. They are also able to reinforce their self-belief through affirmations (in essence, they remind themselves that they are good). Oh, and one other thing. Positive people avoid spending time with negative people. They know that such people don't do them any good. You see, positive and negative moods are contagious.

So when it comes to study and exams, what should you do to generate a positive outlook? I find the following helps:

■ Create and then use a number of affirmations. For example, you could have one in which you tell yourself that you will do well in the exams. For this to work, you will need to repeat the affirmation enough times so that you start to believe it. It might seem odd to begin with, but over time you will begin to believe that you will do well in your exams. And do you know what? You will.

■ Don't get hung up with all the fear and loathing stuff. For example, the next time you start to worry about failure, just recognise the feeling for what it is and remember that the more you try to fight it the worse it becomes. Choose a different response.

■ Turn your face up to the ceiling (so no one can see you) and grin as widely as you can. You can't help but feel more positive doing this, and it certainly works for my kids.

Some courses like to test you using open book exams. Now this might seem like a dream come true, but you'll need to be exceptionally well organised if you are to succeed. IDEA 48, *Open and shut case*, can show you how.

Try another idea...

'My opinions may have changed, but not the fact that I am right.'
ASHLEIGH BRILLIANT, artist, writer and philosophical cartoonist

Defining idea...

83

So how does positive thinking help? There are a number of ways, including the following:

■ It helps you deal with the inevitable setbacks that occur during study and certainly during exams.

■ It keeps your mind open and active, and hence fully productive. Negativity and fear can freeze your power of thought.

■ It allows you to keep focused on your goal of getting good grades.

■ It stops your head from filling up with all those irrational emotions that serve to distract you and undermine your positive energy.

■ It makes you more creative and capable.

■ It allows you to spot opportunities to enhance your study.

■ It makes study far more enjoyable.

Convinced yet? I am. Can't you see my smile?

Q **Are you recommending that I avoid some of my fellow students?**

How did it go?

A *No, that's a little extreme and probably impossible to do, but you might think about spending more time with the positive ones. As I mentioned above, all moods, whether they are positive or negative, are contagious. You certainly don't want to be too near the mood Hoovers near exam time, sucking all your positivity out. You're gonna need all the positive energy you can muster. So hang out with the happy gang.*

Q **Can I get tapes on how to develop positive thinking skills?**

A *You certainly can. There are so many motivational books and audiotapes out there that you are spoilt for choice. Do bear in mind, though, that they can be a bit cheesy. But hey, you're worth it.*

20
Cramming until you drop

Schools which are specifically designed to cram students' minds full of material are all the rage in the Far East. They have an upside and a downside, and they are coming to a city near you soon.

Enter stage right the cramming school. The regime might be tough and the work may be hard, but the results are impressive.

For those students (and their desperate parents) who are concerned about getting into the right school or university, there is an alternative to the mainstream education system, and that's the cram school. The cram school has evolved to fill the gap left by conventional schools and is specifically designed to help students pass all sorts of exams, particularly entrance exams. They are very common in Japan, Korea and Greece, where they almost outnumber state schools. Most cram schools specialise in preparing students either for a particular entrance exam or for a particular subject, such as English, maths or science. There are also schools which are there to help those poor unfortunates who screwed up their exams the first time round. Their approach to getting you through the exams is quite simple: you have to behave like a parrot (minus the perch, of course). No debates, no two-way

Here's an idea for you... **Determine whether a cram school will be of benefit to you. You will need to consider two things. The first is how important the impending exam is to you. If it is critical for your future, and therefore essential that you pass with a high grade, make a provisional tick and go on to question 2, which is: can you afford it? If you have rich parents or a very large piggy bank, then you'll be fine, but such schools do not come cheap.**

flow of ideas, it's time to act like a sponge and then repeat what you have learnt without thinking. The skill of the cram school is to focus on exactly what is required by the exam – nothing more and certainly nothing less.

As you'd expect, there are both upsides and downsides to this cramming school thing. The upsides are obvious. You will move from being a D- or C-grade student to achieving a B or A grade. You will almost certainly get to grips with exam technique, and you might even develop some useful lifelong learning attitudes and behaviours along the way. And it often puts you in a good position for your career. On the downside, these schools can be very expensive. This is because they are privately run. Next, the commitment is significant. It's not unusual to spend up to eighteen hours a day studying if you are at one of these schools full-time; and if you just want to continue your studies after school, you'll still have to put in four or more hours on top of your normal day. A lot of cram schools also provide coverage over the summer holidays and it is normal for students, especially in Japan, to spend the whole of their summer holidays studying in this way. But don't expect a fully rounded education there. If 'irrelevant subjects such as music and art' are taught at the expense of the subjects that matter, students have been known to rebel.

Perhaps the idea of spending eighteen hours a day studying sends shivers down your spine. If it does, get to grips with IDEA 31, *No gain without pain*.

Try another idea...

I must admit, I find this degree of obsession a bit of a turn off. Sure, it's important that you settle down and focus on your studying, but to the detriment of everything else? Surely there ought to be some balance? But hey, it's an idea and even if you or I don't fancy it, it is still popular in certain cultures. And, it's beginning to catch on across the globe, especially as being well educated is the only way to ensure you can get a decent job these days. So expect to see more of the cram school. Who knows, you might end up going to one.

Now you might have figured something out here; well I hope you have. You will have noticed that the cram school is very much associated with the Asian cultures. This is because a student's future is determined by his or her grades and little else, which, in turn, means that entrance exams to the right schools and universities are taken very, very seriously. Western cultures don't place so much importance on education; often, film and pop stars are considered more important. Time to change, perhaps?

'Students who work harder go farther.'
JOANNE JACOBS, American writer and blogger on education

Defining idea...

How did it go?

Q   Where are these cramming schools?

A   Outside of Asia they are fewer in number, but you can normally find some in most cities. The best way to locate them is via the internet. Given they are often run within Asian communities, it is often a good idea to pick up information from local newspapers or talk to members of that community. Word of mouth can help you find out where such schools are and also which ones offer you what you need.

Q   Just how expensive are crammers?

A   You would expect to pay the equivalent of a few hundred to a few thousand dollars, depending on what you need. Courses usually last between six and eight weeks. I've been told by people who have attended such schools that the cost is well worth it.

Q   Can they make a big difference to my academic future?

A   Yes, they can. Some US cram schools boast that large numbers of their students end up at the best universities, like Harvard, Yale and Stanford. Ultimately, though, it all depends on where you want your academic future to go and why. If you've set your sights on a top institution, then maybe a cram school could be a good idea. If you haven't, then maybe not.

21

Hired hand

No matter how good the state system, many people believe that additional support is required if you want to reach for the sky. Tutors are in high demand at every level, from concerned parents to go-getting students.

I have used tutors for myself and for my son. In both instances it did the trick: I achieved the grade I required in complex maths and Tom was able to master the intricacies of the English language and basic maths.

One thing that causes a lot of debate amongst parents, teachers and students is whether or not to employ tutors. There is an ideological argument that says adequate teaching should be available to all and that it is therefore wrong to use the services of these hired hands, but as far as I am concerned, on a more pragmatic level, if they can help you pass exams, then why not? Tutors are invaluable because they can help plug those all-important gaps in your capability and make the difference between a pass and fail, or between an average grade and a top grade. If, like me, you are comfortable with employing tutors, then here are some ground rules which you should find helpful:

- Only use the services of someone who knows their subject. General tutors are fine, but they will never get you to the level of competence that you are

If you want to give a tutor a try, ask one of your existing teachers. They are usually very receptive (they need the cash, you know) and give you some immediate advantages. First, they know you and your learning style and secondly, they will be familiar with your areas of weakness. What's more, they are often much nicer outside of the classroom!

probably looking for. So if you need a geography tutor, make sure you are getting someone who has majored in geography.

- Employ existing teachers/lecturers or someone from an agency: you get more out of experts than you do amateurs. There are plenty of agencies out there who have a portfolio of experts on their books, and this is where I tend to source them. Not only do you end up with a quality individual, but you also have a contract against which you can measure that quality should it fail to meet your expectations.

- Make sure they are up to speed with the syllabus of your exam and the expectations of your examination board. They may be able to teach you all sorts of fascinating and wonderful things, but you'll gain the most value by focusing on the things that matter.

- Be very clear about what you want to use them for. There are two ways you can achieve this. The first is to work on your known areas of weakness with regard to type of question (say, multiple choice) and the second is to focus on those parts of the syllabus which you don't feel very comfortable with.

- Ensure you get plenty of practice with exam questions. I find that this is one of the best uses of the external tutor and one that provides maximum value because they can help you produce model answers.

■ Don't end up with them becoming your crutch. One of the most important things to avoid is using the tutor when you no longer require them. Good ones will let you know when it is time to part company, but it is a good idea to set yourself some targets and, once you have reached them, accept that you no longer require help (it's a bit like therapy, this one).

As the internet has matured, so has the availability and quality of academic material. Log on to IDEA 25, *Surf's up*, for more info.

Try another idea...

If you feel even remotely uneasy about your subject, take a long, hard look at the syllabus and your capabilities. When doing so, you must be brutally honest, as there is no value in deluding yourself. If you find there are gaps in your knowledge, or in your ability to answer some of the questions (which you will need to have noted down from the odd past exam paper or two), jot them down. Once you have a list, prioritise them so that the most critical areas (the ones with the biggest gaps, or where you feel the most exposed) appear first on your list. Then, as you pass down the list, determine how you will plug the gaps. Some might be eliminated by spending a bit more time in the library or drawing on group study. For those where there is no obvious answer, you ought to consider getting hold of a tutor, especially if you are having problems understanding what it's all about. They will advance your comprehension significantly.

Sourcing a tutor is quite straightforward. You can look up tutors in your local yellow pages or you could go online to find one. The main thing is to get one who you are comfortable with, and if it doesn't work out, go find another. In order to get the best from them, make sure your learning objectives are very clear from the start.

'I wish I was as cocksure of anything as Tom Macaulay is of everything.'
LORD MELBOURNE

Defining idea...

How did
it go?

Q   Are tutors value for money?

A   *I believe they are, although you will be the judge of this. But when you are paying a professional's hourly rate, it is important to make sure you are getting what you need out of the relationship. Do this by having very fixed goals before you start.*

Q   Should I have a generalist or specialist?

A   *I prefer to use specialists, as they will have the in-depth knowledge you probably need to master the subject. However, there are odd occasions when a generalist might be more beneficial, especially if it is advice on exam technique that you are really after. The best way to decide is to make a priority list and then work out where you need the most help.*

Q   When should I use the tutor?

A   *Like everything else with studying, there is value to be had by using tutors early on. Spending a few weeks with a tutor during the early stages of your studying will ensure that you are able to commit the learning to your long-term memory. If you start early enough, you will also have plenty of time to employ other tutors for other subjects, if needed. On the other hand, if you use them before you've ascertained whether there's a need, you'll just be wasting money.*

22

Many hands make light work

It can be very lonely studying all by yourself with only the radio for company. Alternatively, group study can be very productive and a lot of fun.

I used to have a great time when it came to group study. We would focus for a few hours before cracking open some beer or going out for a meal. It was always well worth the effort and expense!

I class any study which is not alone as group study. So, even if you study with a partner, as I did with my fiancée, now wife, it still counts because you're not on your lonesome. Once you move beyond your school exams, and particularly when at university, the value of studying in a group cannot be overstated. The benefits are significant and include:

- Accelerating your knowledge. Two brains are always better than one because the other person will bring different perspectives, fresh ideas and some much needed challenge which only serves to expand your knowledge horizons.

Speak to your fellow students and see if they are interested in running a few group study sessions. Trial one out to see if it works and then, based upon the results, improve it so that everyone gets some benefit.

■ Focusing more than one head on coursework. Having more than one person working on an assignment allows you to break up the work and swap ideas about how best to answer the question.

■ Exploring difficult areas of the syllabus. Few of us could claim to know the syllabus inside out, and most of us tend to favour some topics over others. So if you are struggling with a particular area it is highly likely that one of your fellow students will know it better than you.

■ Testing each other when it comes to revision time. Bringing a group together to dissect exam questions and swap ideas on how they can be answered can save you a lot of heartache.

One of the major benefits I received through group study was the recognition that we were all in the same boat. It's easy to believe that everyone else is faring better than you, until you ask. Then you find that most people share the same hopes and fears about studying and you immediately have a support network which you can draw on when the going gets tough. Once established, it is a great way to remove some of the blocks that arise from time to time.

Although a group study session can take on many forms, I would recommend that you try the following. Set aside an afternoon when your study-mates are also available. Prior to meeting up, decide on the topic area, or areas, you are going to concentrate on. As preparation, ask everyone who attends (which should probably be four or five) to identify those parts of the syllabus they are having difficulty with and the questions they would like answered. When you meet up, begin by listing everyone's issues and questions, and then group them together to see if you can identify any common patterns. Having completed this, agree which ones you are going to focus on for the session. This is important because there are likely to be more topics than time available. The best way to prioritise is to select those topics which most of the group are struggling with or which could yield the greatest benefits. For each of the topic areas you are going to cover, create a question which the group should debate and explore. Feel free to draw on any books, lecture notes, exam papers or anything else that will help. As you discuss the topic, have someone capture the key points, messages, examples and suggested structure for answering the question. If possible, do this electronically, or choose the person with the neatest handwriting – just so long as it's legible. Once you have exhausted the topic, move onto the next, and so on until time is up. At the end of the session, have someone briefly summarise the group's work and agree on how the notes are going to be distributed (email, photocopy, etc.).

To make a group study session work, so that everyone feels they are benefiting from the process, you need to play by some important rules. Here are the ones I use:

- Ensure that everyone is given airtime.

- Listen to a person's point of view without interrupting (no matter how tempting!).

- Be willing to provide support for those amongst the group who may be struggling.

Many of us now choose to follow distance learning courses. These have developed significantly in the last few years, so to find out what they entail, go to IDEA 30, *Earth calling*.

Try another idea...

'*The miracle is – the more we share the more we have.*'
OVID

Defining idea...

97

- Provide constructive criticism when it is invited, remembering to point out what is good as well as what could be improved.

- Take a break when the energy levels begin to drop. Have a cup of coffee, a stretch or some fresh air for 15 minutes.

Q   **Isn't group study just an excuse to switch off and have a laugh?**

A   *It's true, there is always a risk that everyone will relax too much and socialise instead of studying. The way to avoid this is to have a specific objective to work to and to take responsibility for your own discipline.*

Q   **How long should we spend on each group session?**

A   *This depends a little bit on numbers, but assuming there are no more than six of you, I would recommend something in the region of 1–3 hours. Naturally, if you are attempting to tackle a particularly difficult part of the syllabus, you should take a bit longer.*

Q   **How often should we run them?**

A   *Once you have got a good study group established, I would be tempted to run one every couple of weeks. And in the run up to the exams I would hold them once or twice a week. They can be a real confidence boost.*

23

Round, round, I get around

Most people tend to be somewhat passive when it comes to their study, which makes the whole process boring and a turn off. To keep your study both interesting and alive it is a good idea to use active revision techniques.

What do you prefer: poring over copious notes time after time or using lists, summaries, diagrams and other more active approaches to get all that information into your skull? For a long time I was a passive studier. Not any more, though.

Experts recommend that we should make our study as active as possible. Apparently, passive techniques, which typically involve reading notes over and over again, only allow us to *recognise* the material we have read. To do well in our exams we need to be able to *recall* the information we have collected during our formal lessons, practicals and tutorials, and the only way we can achieve this is through employing active techniques. There is a difference between recognising information and recalling it: if you recognise information, you can regurgitate it in the same form as you absorbed it; if you recall it, as you are often required to do during an exam, you will be able to draw upon your knowledge, apply it and present it in a

Here's an idea for you... **List out the subjects you are currently studying on one side of a page of A4 (or equivalent) paper. Then for each subject select a different active study technique. This will help to build in some variety and will allow you to keep your brain interested as you switch from one subject to another.**

different way in order to answer the question. And in order to be able to do this, you have to get used to using it in different ways, hence the need to use active techniques. So what techniques can we use? I like the following:

- Create mind maps. This, by using the right and left sides of your brain together, mimics the way the brain links information.

- Make key notes, which involves distilling your lectures and tutorials to a small number of key words which you can then use for revision purposes.

- Produce lists of key facts, figures and sound bites associated with a particular topic.

- Create relationship diagrams which allow you to link discrete blocks of information together. These are distinct from mind maps in that they allow you to link quite separate concepts together, as opposed to build on a subject as you would in mind mapping.

- Create outline answers based upon real questions found in past papers.

- Develop checklists of key questions and the information required to answer them.

Once you have gone through the process of distilling your lectures to a set of useful notes, try this two-step process, which seems to work for a lot of people I have talked to. Step one involves posing yourself a series of questions which will force you to bring out the knowledge you have just committed to paper. If you prefer, you can use real exam questions from past papers, though to a large extent it is unimportant at this stage. Then, instead of sitting down and writing your answers, walk around your room, or outside if it's sunny, and recall the answers verbally.

The mind and body are more closely linked than many people think. In fact, your mind can effectively shut down if your body is tired. As IDEA 29, *Mind, body and spirit*, shows, to get the most of out of study you need to get your body active too.

Try another idea...

There are two advantages to this approach. First, because you are moving around your physiology will help to keep your frontal lobes open and accessible, and your mind will be more active. Secondly, it helps to create and reinforce synaptic links within your brain. These links become stronger the more they are repeated, so you should repeat the process a few times to ensure that the links are good enough to enable the effective recall of information.

It's also useful to remember that boys and girls learn differently. Whereas girls prefer to sit quietly and absorb things through reading and listening to their tutors, boys would rather be putting their learning into a practical frame. So if you're a guy reading this, think about how to make your learning practical. For example, if you are studying history, you could consider visiting a key battlefield and walking around it with a guide. This will bring an otherwise one-dimensional text to life and help to reinforce your learning. And if you're a woman, read on, or go along for the ride and enjoy the day out while he catches up with you.

'The world can only be grasped by action, not by contemplation...The hand is the cutting edge of the mind.'
JACOB BRONOWSKI

Defining idea...

How did
it go?

Q   Should I give up on producing detailed notes?

A   *Not at all. You will need to create a solid foundation on which you can base your active revision, and the only way to achieve this is to create a comprehensive set of notes. So you will have to trawl through all that material after all. But on the plus side, you may only have to do it once.*

Q   Which technique should I use?

A   *Before you settle on a particular technique, you might want to explore a few. So give mind mapping a go, key words, question spotting, practice questions, and so on. You will soon settle on those that you are most comfortable with. The key thing is that you will have made your study active. If you find that you prefer only one or two techniques, then that's fine. Just because they are available doesn't mean that you have to use them all.*

Q   Could I use a tape recorder?

A   *Yes, this is another way to make your study active. Why not tape yourself reading your notes and then, as you go to bed, play it back to yourself. As well as absorbing the notes subliminally, you'll probably send yourself to sleep in next to no time! And we all know how important a good night's sleep is.*

24
All work and no play

Focus, focus, focus. Some folks believe that the only way to pass exams and complete their studies is to work, work, work. No time for rest, and certainly no time for play. Is this a good strategy? Psychologists don't think so.

To study effectively, you need to break that seemingly endless task into bite-sized portions. Too much studying without a rest is unproductive, and will probably cause you to fall short in your exams. So, cut yourself some slack and take some time out.

Taking holidays from work and study should be an essential part of our routine. It is well known that holidays and periods of rest have a significant restorative effect on our bodies. And studies have shown that so long as these are of a minimum duration of seven days, the effects last longer than just for the holiday itself. The beauty of holidays is that they allow you to completely switch off and do something completely different, whether that's visiting new places, reading books or just

Here's an idea for you... **If you are one who loves sport, try to build it into the beginning and end of your study week. Start Monday off with a couple of hours of sport and finish it with a couple of hours on a Friday afternoon. The Monday session will get you in a great frame of mind to study by getting your body pumped up and Friday's will help clear your mind before the weekend, when you can relax a bit.**

relaxing on a beach. By switching off you are also allowing your brain to absorb and make sense of the information you have been throwing into it during the course of your study. It's very important to give your brain time to make connections between the individual pieces of data. In this regard, the brain is like a filing cabinet. If you just shove everything at the front, come the time you want to retrieve something it takes you ages to put your hands on it. But stored logically in the right place, you can go straight to the item with out any deviation. I certainly find that a period of relaxation or even a train journey gives the grey cells the time they need to make sense of everything. In fact, train journeys are where I get most of my inspiration for the simple reason that I have nothing else to do.

Of course, it's not just holidays that are important; the time you spend with your friends and family is just as crucial in ensuring that you maintain a sensible balance in your life. As well as providing more diverse stimulation, they can also provide support and reassurance, and revitalise your positive outlook on life.

Another thing to remember is that you need to give yourself rewards for all the hard work you have been doing. The best way to do this is to set yourself some targets, such as learning about a specific topic or completing a sample exam question, and then, once you have achieved it, reward yourself by having some fun. Key to making this successful is not to reward yourself before you have met the objective. So sit down with a diary and block out some time in which you will do anything but study. You will need to be disciplined about this, so make sure it's

One way to break up the monotony of study is to go for spells in the library. See IDEA 7, _Books, glorious books_, to see why the library is such a great resource.

Try another idea...

something that will be difficult to cancel. For example, you could meet someone for lunch, or book some cinema or theatre tickets. The weekend is another good time to block out. Try to plan the odd weekend away with family or friends. Not only will you feel good because you've just spent some quality time with your loved ones, you'll be able go back to your studies refreshed and raring to go.

You may find that you just don't have the time for rest and relaxation. I won't lecture you here, but it's vital that you at least do something, because otherwise you'll get tired and unproductive. Then you could be in real danger of falling into a vicious circle of studying for even longer because you don't feel you are being productive enough. Time out ensures you are more productive, not less. So even if you are not going to go down the pub or the cinema, try some of the following:

- Meditation. Spend a few minutes with the curtains drawn and your eyes shut, and focus your mind on things other than your studies. Apparently, focusing on your breathing alone will reduce your stress levels and make you more productive.

'**All work and no play makes Jack a dull boy.**'
17th CENTURY PROVERB

Defining idea...

105

- Yoga. I personally love this. A bit painful at first, but well worth it. A few stretches will make your brain jump into action.

- Shutting your eyes and visualising a happy memory.

- Day dreaming about your future, perhaps even completing the exam successfully if you really want to!

- Power napping. Much favoured by high-powered executives, this seems to revitalise even the most stressed out and tired worker bee. If it works for them, I'm sure it will work for you.

So instead of grabbing another large latte, try something different.

Q How much time should I take off between sessions?

A As a general rule you should aim to have regular breaks every one to two hours. These breaks should be of a minimum duration of 30 minutes. So go and make yourself a coffee, speak to your flatmates or listen to the radio for a while. Better still, go out and get some fresh air. Also, if you are studying all week, you should take the weekend off to recharge your batteries, and if you have been studying for long periods, such as a few weeks solid, then you ought to take a week or so off to get away from it completely.

Q I don't feel that I have the time to take a week off. What should I do?

A The best thing to do is to jot down your subjects and list any outstanding areas which you still need to cover. Then, using a diary, work back from the exam dates and assess whether you will be able to complete them in time. You will probably find that you have plenty of opportunities to take some time off. And if you are this organised, you probably deserve it.

Q Should I take a block of time off just before my exams?

A This all depends on how comfortable you feel. If you believe you have mastered your subjects and are confident that you have done as much as you can, a brief holiday before the exams isn't a bad thing. If you are one for last-minute revision, then you might want to spend a little bit more time working before allowing yourself some rest!

How did
it go?

107

25

Surf's up

The internet provides a fantastic resource for anyone wishing to augment their study, so it's no wonder there are so many opportunities to both study and gain qualifications online.

You often only hear about the internet in relation to studying when some kid has downloaded an essay and handed it in as all her own work. Assuming you are honest enough not to do that, the internet is a great way to enhance your study.

The internet provides a huge resource for those undertaking any form of study. No longer restricted to libraries and books, the internet allows you to share knowledge and learn from others more rapidly than ever before. With millions of sites dedicated to single subjects, chat rooms where it is possible to swap ideas and offer advice, and online universities and learning resources providing distance learning via the web, learning has never been easier, no matter what you are studying.

Here's an idea for you...

If you are planning to use your computer a lot, make sure your study environment is set up to avoid the most common computer-related health problems (or terminal illnesses). So build breaks into your regime to avoid eye and muscle strain; ensure there is plenty of light in your room; position yourself so that your arms are horizontal and you are 350–600 mm away from the screen; and try and keep your wrists straight. A good posture is critical to a productive working environment, so invest in a good desk and adjustable chair.

Moreover, the internet provides a rich environment that can bring the learning process alive with a mix of graphics, self-assessments, video, audio and real-time interaction. One of my colleagues is studying for his Masters degree and all of it is done online, from the electronic books through to his interactions with his tutors. It's amazing: no contact whatsoever; ideal for a recluse or somebody whose body clock is attuned to a different continent's time zone. The internet offers the student the following:

- Access to lecture notes, revision guides and other reading material, which you can easily add to and tailor to your specific requirements. This can be a real advantage to the disorganised student and will certainly help when it comes to revising.

- Interactive tools, which can include online presentations, video clips and tests. Online tests are particularly helpful where they exist, as you are able to get some real-time feedback on your performance.

- Online tutor support and feedback, which can be at any time of the day. Some schemes provide 24/7 support, whereby tutors around the globe collaborate to provide you with support no matter what your local time is. So if you wake up in the middle of the night worrying about a particular topic, you could always log on and send off a query.

Are you coming back to studying after a long break? If so, you would be wise to have a look at IDEA 1, _Are you sitting comfortably?_

Try another idea...

- Student networks, where you can collaborate with your fellow students in a virtual environment. This can be great for group projects and when revising.

- Webinars, where students can log onto a predefined website and listen to the lecture whilst seeing the slides appear on their computer. They can also ask the lecturer questions by typing them into their computer. It's just like being in a lecture theatre but you can attend in your pyjamas!

Making the most of the electronic environment requires you to apply some common sense because there is so much material out there. You can spend so many hours searching for material that you may not get down to the actual hard graft of studying, which is committing all the information to your long-term memory. So be very clear on what you are trying to find (an example, a sample answer, an exam paper and so on) and then be selective on how you use the Net. The best thing to do is to find the best sites, chat rooms, tutor sites and so on and stick to these. After all, if it works, there's no need to look elsewhere.

'e-learning is not about computers and is not about computing.'
ELLIOTT MASIE, futurist

Defining idea...

111

How did it go?

Q   If the electronic channel is that good, can I skip lectures?

A   *Well, most students do anyway, don't they? Seriously, most courses require you to attend some face-to-face lessons, and you will be required to work in groups. So although you may feel that you could get through the course without any physical contact, there is much value to be had from interacting with other people. The other thing to remember is that it can take hours and hours to find what you really need from the Net. At least in lectures it is given to you without you having to locate it first.*

Q   How computer literate do I need to be?

A   *You can get by with only the minimum of computer literacy these days. Long gone are the days when you had to know how to build a computer from first principles. As long as you have some basic keyboard skills, know how to surf the internet and can use some of the common packages such as Microsoft Word, then you'll be just fine. You can always take a crash course in computer usage if you are worried.*

Q   Can I use the ready-made model answers from the internet?

A   *You can, but it's important to remember the purpose of following any course: it's for you to learn something. One danger of relying on ready-made answers – from the internet or anywhere else – is that you don't need to think about what you are writing. Then when it's exam time and a question requires something more than your model answer, you're up the proverbial creek with a mouse for a paddle.*

26
Blueprint for success

Feeling prepared for the exam is a good feeling, but if you want to be even more prepared, one of the best ways is to build some model answers. These can be particularly helpful in exams where essays are required.

I learnt the power of the model answer a long time ago, when I had a great idea for an essay about the First World War. I developed the structure, the characters and the plot so that, no matter what the question, I was able to twist the answer to fit like a glove.

Not all exams suit the model answer approach, so it is worth running through your subjects to see which ones do. In the main, any subject which requires discussion in the form of an essay could be a good target for this approach. English Language is a great favourite of mine, as you are usually given a free rein to write about whatever you like. So long as you can twist your model answer to the title you are given, you can whiz through the question without having to give it enormous amounts of thought. This can save you large chunks of time.

Having built your model answer (or answers, if you want to hedge your bets a bit), pick up two exam papers and, under exam conditions, see if you can complete an answer using your model. If you can, that's great, but if you can't, don't worry; just go back to your material to see if you have missed anything. If it has worked, check it over with one of your tutors to see how complete the answer is. Better still, ask her to mark it for you. Feedback is important here, so grab it if you can.

One way in which you can build up your model answers is to trawl through some past papers. This will give you an indication of the type of questions that come up and what kind of answers they are looking for, and hence what information you need to answer them. Once you have had a good look through the papers, spend a bit of time developing the kernel of a model answer. This should consist of the key facts and figures, major points of view that should be made, primary conclusions and other supporting material you feel you may need. Next, draw up a matrix of each exam question and identify where each element of the model answer could fit. Having populated the matrix, review the results to see if you are missing anything. If you are, go back to your sources and gather some more information, facts, figures, etc. Ideally you should be aiming to cover as much of the matrix with a single answer as possible.

Of course, model answers are not just for essays: they can be used for the derivation of mathematical formulae or scientific proofs. The fundamental difference here is that there will be less flexibility in its application. So, if you believe that you will be expected to derive the formula for the volume of a cone, as I once did, build up the answer from first principles. Once you have created the answer you will need to memorise it so that you can recall it should it appear. The best way to do this is to derive it without notes a few times under exam conditions. And to make sure it is really buttoned down, create a mental cue that will allow you to bring it out with ease.

The real benefit of having a model answer up your sleeve is that it can provide an amazing boost to your confidence. It's a great feeling to spot a question which you know you can answer without having to put in a huge effort. If you do spot one, then you should always tackle it first. There are two reasons for this: first, it gets the first question out of the way and some decent points in the bag; and secondly, because you can reel it off it is likely to buy you some valuable time which you could profitably spend on a much trickier question.

We all struggle with the amount of information we are expected to learn during studying and recall during the exams. Creating memory stacks is a highly effective and fun way to achieve this. To learn more, go see IDEA 36, *Stacking the shelves.*

Try another idea...

'Excellence is to do a common thing in an uncommon way.'
BOOKER T. WASHINGTON

Defining idea...

How did it go?

Q   **Couldn't I come unstuck if my model answer doesn't fit the question?**

A   *Of course, there is always a risk. Reducing the likelihood of the model answer failing to hit the mark involves building in enough richness. In other words, incorporating extra information into the model can give you the leeway of cutting bits out when flexing the model answer under exam conditions.*

Q   **Can you apply the model to more than one question?**

A   *Sure you can, but you shouldn't expect one model to fit all answers. I generally work on the basis that a single model should be used for one answer, and if you can bend it to any other then that should be considered a bonus. I was once lucky enough to have one model answer fit two questions during one exam, which was very fortunate, if very rare.*

Q   **Can I base my study on just model answers?**

A   *If only life were that simple! Because exams are not entirely predictable, I would advise you to use model answers as part of your overall strategy. Using a variety of techniques will provide you with the necessary diversity to keep you interested and engaged, and will also give you the confidence you need in the exam hall to deal with whatever the examiners throw at you.*

27
Night boat to Cairo

You'd never believe that a pyramid had much to do with studying, would you? But it does. Just look at its shape.

It's always tempting to pack as much as you can into your essay to demonstrate that you know your subject. The problem is that you can lose sight of the most important part: the conclusion.

The key to success here is to start with your conclusion and work backwards. This is the pyramid principle.

Barbara Minto first came up with the concept of the pyramid principle whilst working for McKinsey & Company. As the first woman consultant with a particular skill in writing, she was asked to develop the writing abilities of the other consultants. It transpired that it wasn't the writing skills *per se* that needed improving, but the thinking skills required to create clear and well-structured reports. The art of a good report, essay or any other kind of written work depends on separating the thinking process from the writing process so that the thinking part is completed before the writing part begins. I've lost count of the number of

Take an exam question and write it as you normally would. Take as long as you need and, once you have finished it, put it to one side. Then repeat the exercise, but this time use the pyramid principle to structure and then answer the question. Once you have finished both essays, give them to a friend or, if you are feeling very brave, your tutor and ask him to read them both and score them out of ten in terms of structure, readability and impact. The results should amaze you and will demonstrate the power of the principle.

times I've launched straight into an exam question without formally thinking about what I was going to write, and I'm sure I'm not the only one. Separating the thinking from the writing not only helps you to create a well-structured answer, but it also helps your reader (i.e. the examiner) understand more readily what you are trying to convey. So how do you apply the principle? Like this:

- Start by sorting the information into logical groupings, which is the way the mind works anyway. (When the mind is confronted with a set of seemingly unrelated items it will attempt to create relationships and group them logically.) So if you had a list of words which included a variety of insects, mammals and birds, you would automatically start to brigade all insects under an insect heading, all the mammals under a mammal heading and the same with the birds. Presented graphically, this hierarchy would look like a pyramid. 'Coincidence?' I hear you ask.

- Having established the relationships between the various pieces of information, you now need to decide on the order in which you are going to present them. The best way to do this is to begin with the summarised idea. This plays on the readers' ability to take in whole sentences at a time, and avoids them spending too much time and mental capacity on recognising and interpreting the words and building the relationships between them. By presenting the summarised idea first, you give them more time to comprehend the significance of what you are saying. Presenting your ideas in a pyramid fashion allows them to comprehend what the message is with the minimum of effort.

- Finally you will need to develop your ideas in a bottom-up way. Although you will present your final ideas top-down, you need to group the related concepts and sub-concepts from the bottom up so that they support the next level up in the hierarchy.

If you take a simple essay, where you are expected to come up with a conclusion about the merits of, let's say, John F. Kennedy and how he handled the Cuban Missile Crisis, you would need to structure your essay in the following way:

- Start with the conclusion about J.F.K., which might be that he showed great leadership during the Cuban Missile Crisis.

- Next, present your sub-conclusions that support this top-level conclusion. These will be the statements that demonstrate J.F.K.'s leadership skills in the context of the Bay of Pigs. Each sub-conclusion should be dealt with separately.

'*To climb steep hills requires a slow pace at first.*'
SHAKESPEARE

Defining idea…

119

■ Then you can provide further elaboration on each of the sub-conclusions by building up paragraphs which sustain the argument and the statements you have made.

The way to view such a structure is as presenting your most important argument first and then breaking it down to provide the necessary support. It will appear very logical to the reader and as a result simpler to read.

Q Can you apply this principle to any question?

A It can be used whenever you need to provide a written answer, whether it's a short comprehension question or a long essay.

Q I am struggling with building the concept; do you have any more hints?

A Minto offers three rules, which I find helpful. The first is that any idea you represent must be supported by, the ideas below them. The second is that each idea within a group must be related to each other idea. And finally, they must be logically ordered so that the ideas are in their natural order.

Q Where should I start?

A Like all exam and revision techniques, you always have to start with your base material.

28

Last orders, please

What do you prefer: a well-formulated plan mapped out well in advance, or waiting until a few days before the exam before knuckling down to study? Many people prefer the latter, but it's risky, and not so smart if you want to do well.

It's a funny thing, last-minute revision. Having done it once I can attest to its value, but also to the seat-of-the-pants feeling as you walk into the exam hall. It worked for me then, but it's a high-risk strategy.

There is nothing wrong with the concept of last-minute revision so long as it is part of a coherent study strategy. From my experience, and from other last-minuters I have talked to, it seems to work. However, if you are choosing the last-minute route because you can't be bothered to spend a couple of months before the exam learning about your subject, then I don't think it's such a great idea. In fact, you can usually spot those who have adopted this approach by their vacant expressions during the exam and their early departure from the examination hall! Those who

If you decide that last-minute revision is for you, go about it the following way. First you need to put it into the context of the exam. So sit down with the syllabus, a couple of past exam papers and all the resources you need to access (books, the internet and your notes are a good start) and decide which topics to concentrate on. Then focus on those topics for periods of only one hour. Once the hour is up, stop and take a break. After your break, see how much of this material you can recall and then focus on those bits you failed to remember. Cramming last thing at night is recommended, as you'll remember more in the morning.

use a combination of structured and last-minute study often fair pretty well, especially when this is balanced across a number of topic areas.

Although many students go for the last-minute cramming approach – whether through necessity or through choice – psychologists believe it to be one of the least valuable methods of study. This is because there are limits to one's short-term memory, which can last for only a few scant seconds or minutes. So to be truly successful you must have committed most of the information you'll be drawing on to your long-term memory. If you've done this, then topping-up with a bit of short-term memory can't harm. The fundamental difference between short-term and long-term memory is that the former is just memorisation whilst the latter is about understanding. What's more, the longer you think about a subject, the more of it gets committed to your long-term memory. So time is key, but don't overdo it as I used to – a fifty-two-week study regime is possibly giving yourself a little bit more time than you will really need!

Another thing to remember about the last-minute cramming approach is to ensure that you get enough sleep. Studying 24/7 for a few days before the exam may allow you to force as much material into your head as possible, but you will soon become very tired. If you go into the exam without having had sufficient sleep you increase your chances of making silly mistakes. The other interesting thing is that sleeping longer will allow more information to be absorbed and will allow you to remember more. So make sure that you intersperse your cramming sessions with rest breaks and ensure you leave yourself sufficient time for sleep. The other thing to remember is that, because you haven't left yourself much time, your notes need to be brief and as condensed as possible. Not only will you not have time to remember anything but the shortest notes, you won't have time to make huge piles of them anyway.

If the idea of learning everything that has been taught to you turns you cold, why not consider question spotting? Go to IDEA 13, *Spotting the winners*, to spot the answers.

Try another idea...

'Ah! The clock is always slow; It's later than you think.'
ROBERT W. SERVICE

Defining idea...

How did
it go?

Q   I like the idea of last-minute study, so shouldn't I do it?

A   I'm not suggesting that you should ignore the value that cramming provides, but rather that it should not be relied on exclusively. You are better off combining it with something with a bit more structure. I recommend that you work out which topics you can get away with cramming and those which will require some more time (and effort) to get ready for the exam and plan accordingly

Q   If I'm going to go for the last-minute approach, how late should I leave it?

A   The simple answer is not too late! It is not generally a good idea to leave your studying until the day before the exam (although I have known people who have). You are better off leaving it no later than 3–4 weeks before, as this will give you sufficient time for the information to reach your long-term memory.

Q   Is there a better way?

A   Yes. If you want to cram, then why not consider joining the many students who attend cramming schools during the last vacation before their exams. These provide an environment in which you can undertake intensive revision classes to bring yourself up to a suitable level where you can pass. Typically run on a residential basis with teachers on hand all day, they are an excellent way to build knowledge and confidence simultaneously. The other advantage that these schools provide is the discipline which most crammers lack. So you never know, it might rub off!

124

29

Mind, body and spirit

Your physiology affects your brain along with the rest of your body. If you feel down, your brain doesn't function at its full capacity; conversely, if you feel great, your brain can tackle seemingly impossible tasks.

Play from a 10, I was advised by a personal coach not long ago. My initial response was 'Do what?', but having had the concept explained to me, I felt enlightened and ready to take on the world — playing from a 10.

Now, studying is not necessarily taking on the world, but at times it can certainly seem like it.

Motivation is the bedrock to successful study, and the only person in charge of your motivation is you (sorry about that; you can't blame your teachers, parents or partner). Because no one else is involved with this, we have to become expert at understanding our motivations and harnessing them when we need to. Your ability to motivate yourself depends on your belief system, which determines how you feel about things and therefore how you approach certain things in life, including study. So, if you feel that studying is a waste of time, hey presto! It will be. You will find it boring,

Here's an idea for you... **Sit on a chair and close your eyes. Slouch, with your shoulders hunched and your spine curved. How does it make you feel? Energetic? Resourceful? Full of the joys of spring? Probably not. Now sit bolt upright, with your back straight and shoulders back. Makes you feel a whole lot better and ready to tackle anything, doesn't it? This simple exercise demonstrates just how powerfully your physiology affects the way you feel.**

unproductive and utterly pointless. Of course, your exam results will reflect this attitude. Alternatively, if you believe that study can be fun and enriching, then it will be so. You will find it interesting and informative, and your results will reflect this enthusiasm. Simple, really.

But there is more to it than this, as our general state (and particularly happiness) depends on three things:

■ How much pleasure we have.

■ How much displeasure we experience.

■ How satisfied we feel.

The interesting thing is that, in order to be satisfied and happy, you have to be willing to pass through a certain amount of displeasure first; it is this that makes the end result more satisfying. Studying is difficult and hard, but when you have passed all your exams just think how satisfied and hence happy you'll feel. Without the displeasure, you would not feel the joy of success.

Taking all this together and boiling it down means that in simple terms our effectiveness depends almost entirely on the state we are in – our mental condition. It is this that controls what we feel and how we tackle (i.e. respond to) the situations we face. We can use a simple scale which goes from 0 to 10, with 0 being the lowest performing state and 10 the highest. None of us stays at a single state all of the time, and we should expect it to fluctuate over the course of a day, a week and a year. Being able to control your state is very powerful because it helps you pull out of those more negative moments you'll find yourself in during prolonged studying (i.e. when you are at a zero). Tuning in to how you feel at any given moment and changing it to something more positive can be highly beneficial and will help you be much nearer a 10.

Another way in which you can get into a positive mindset is to be on top of the syllabus. IDEA 2, *Syllabus savvy*, will show you it's not an impossible climb.

Try another idea...

There is a strong association between our psychological state and our physical state; indeed, physiology can dramatically improve our ability to learn. According to the latest research, our ability to master and remember new things is improved by the biological changes in the brain brought about by physical activity. Physical exercise can result in better and healthier brains, which in turn means we are better equipped to learn. It is also well known that when we are anxious our frontal lobes shut down, which limits our ability to reason and address complex issues. The opposite is true when we are happy. Taking this one step further involves creating what is known as an anchor. An anchor is a mental image, word or other cue which we associate with a high performing state. Your anchor can be anything you like: an image from your past, a phrase that you can really associate with or just a particular stance you may hold. (Just make sure it's something you can do without embarrassment in public.) Associating this image with a 10 means that every time you want to be at a high performing state all you need to do is recall the image, replay the phrase or get into that position.

Obviously it takes practice and plenty of repetition to make this an automatic response, but once you've mastered it, you'll be able to play from a 10...instantly.

'Don't be afraid to be amazing.'
ANDY OFFUTT IRWIN, songwriter and storytelling

Defining idea...

127

Q **Are you suggesting that I need to keep in top physical as well as mental condition?**

    A *I think the evidence suggests that it is a good idea. Now I am not suggesting that you become an Olympic athlete, or that all Olympic athletes are great learners, but I am recommending that you get some physical exercise in amongst all your studying. Your state is affected by the amount of endorphins running through your bloodstream, and the best way to get those is through physical exercise. For example, whenever I find myself struggling with study, I go out fencing, and that always helps.*

    Q **How can I maintain a 10?**

    A *Your ability to maintain a high performing state depends on your ability to turn it on when you need it. So you need to create an effective anchor which you associate with your high performing state, and you need to practise using it so that it is easy for you to switch it on.*

    Q **Could I use this technique during my exams?**

    A *Absolutely. The key to being able to use this effectively is to have your high performing anchor always ready for use so that you can turn it on whenever you need. So you could use it whilst waiting to enter the exam hall, or when you are in the exam itself. I have, and it really works.*

30

Earth calling

An increasing number of people follow courses from the comfort of their own home. Distance learning is a great way to study, but it is very different from what you might have been used to.

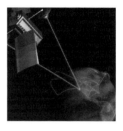

I learnt to juggle by correspondence course. Every two weeks I'd received the next stage of the course, including diagrams, balls and instructions. Within eight weeks I could juggle and could even do some quite fancy moves!

Each of us has a preference when it comes to learning, and this affects how we learn and what environment we prefer to be in. Many of us cannot spare the time (or the money these days) to follow a full-time course, given work commitments and hectic home lives. It's not surprising, then, that the number of institutions offering distance learning as an alternative has increased dramatically. Distance learning has evolved considerably since the early days of the Open University. Today it is truly multimedia, using a combination of traditional book-based work, videos, television programmes (which you can record), audiotapes, the internet and summer schools (where you will be able to meet your fellow students and get to work on some

Here's an idea for you...

If you intend to follow a distance learning course it's a good idea to list all the things that need to be in place to make it a success. So, before you start, jot down your requirements under the following headings: technology, software, environment, support and contact. Then identify how they are going to be satisfied. Now you are in a position to get the best out of your course.

assignments together). Some recent research into the make-up of successful distance learning students shows that you need some quite different attributes from the standard student if you are going to succeed. These are:

■ Real completer-finisher skills – it's a lot harder getting the job done and finishing your assignment outside of an academic environment, so if you are going to follow a distance learning course you need to be particularly good at this.

■ Being comfortable with working under your own steam, with limited direction. This is not to say that you need to be a loner if you are going to do distance learning, just that it helps.

■ Discipline. Remember, there won't be anyone badgering you to go to your room and study, or to finish that essay that's been lying on your desk for weeks. To be successful you will need the discipline to study on a regular basis so that it becomes a habit.

■ A real desire to pass your exams. This may seem quite surprising at first sight, but there are more distractions to overcome in distance learning so you have to be strongly motivated.

So you have all the personal attributes to make distance learning a success; what else do you need to do to ensure that you come away with the result you want? The myriad of study skills that apply to traditional courses come to mind, but what are the key things you need to be especially watchful of? Well, first you will need to create some interim deadlines and goals against which you can track progress and maintain momentum and enthusiasm. Unlike face-to-face courses, you won't have the weekly timetable or lecturers to keep you on the straight and narrow. Instead, it will be down to you, so creating these milestones will be important. Secondly, you will need more quiet time than on traditional courses. Remember that you will need to listen to tapes, spend time on the internet and watch videos. All of these things should be done with the minimum of disruption. So establishing and maintaining a good study environment is probably more critical than normal, and this extends to the availability and reliability of the technologies you'll need to support you, like video recorders and tape players. Thirdly, keep in touch with your tutor. This is vital if you are to clarify what's required of you and your assignments, as well as seeking regular feedback on progress. In many respects you are in the driving seat, so it'll be up to you to seek input when you need it. Fortunately with the internet this is much simpler these days. Finally it's a good idea to create a support network of fellow students. Most courses can help you to establish a network of students in your area, and most encourage it. You will be surprised at just how many other people are pursuing the same course as you, and getting together to discuss it is a great way to keep yourself going. In addition, always attend any planned physical contact with the tutors and fellow

If you want to get the most out of your studying, go to IDEA 5, *Charting your success*, to find out how to use a study charter.

Try another idea...

'*Learning is not compulsory...neither is survival.*'
W. EDWARDS DEMMING

Defining idea...

131

students, such as summer schools. These are a must.

Q   What sort of courses can I do?

A   *These days you can follow a huge variety of courses, from MBAs through to more vocational subjects, such as accounting. If you are considering a distance learning course, check out the main providers to see what's on offer. Most will also indicate the commitment required to complete the course, which you need to consider quite carefully.*

Q   Can I complete the course in my own time?

A   *Yes, pretty much so, though there may be some exceptions – but even these will give you a very generous deadline. This is probably one of the biggest benefits of the distance learning approach, as you can fit your studying in around your other commitments. In some cases students can take five years to finish a degree that could be done on campus in three. Now that's what I call staying power. The pace you work at will be dependent on a number of factors: your work and family situations, and the purpose behind you taking it in the first place.*

Q   How is a distance learning course perceived?

A   *This varies. In the main they are perceived as the poor relation to on-campus courses, mainly because they are believed to be less demanding. I actually think that any course of study is demanding in its own right and, if anything, distance learning requires higher levels of persistence and tenacity than traditional face-to-face programmes. Your choice of whether to complete a course through the distance learning route depends on so many things, all of which are in your control. So you decide.*

31

No gain without pain

Study is no picnic and for most of us it is very painful. But without the pain there can be no gain. It wasn't meant to be easy, you know!

From an early age we learn the difference between pleasure and pain, then spend our lives trying to maximise one and avoid the other. It's no surprise, then, that we all tend to avoid studying and exams. But help is at hand.

Many of our responses to life's events are hard wired. If, for example, you were faced by a ferocious lion I'm pretty certain that you would run away very fast. You certainly wouldn't stand around contemplating the state of the lion's coat or the lovely colour of its eyes. This flight or fight response has been genetically ingrained into us from our ancestors. In the same way, we are conditioned to avoid things that give us pain and seek out stuff which makes us feel good. Therefore, when faced with a situation that involves pain, whether it is real or perceived, your instinctive response is to do everything in your power to avoid it. You will make excuses, find something else to do and generally find the path of least resistance. How many times have you left your assignment to the last minute, or left it too late to really

Take a few minutes to think about how your perception of pleasure and pain links to study and exams. If it is study and exams = pain and free time = pleasure, you need to think about switching them over (well, at least on the days you ought to be studying). The key to making this successful is to project the pleasure (or pain) of your choice of action (delay, or getting on with it) from the future to the present. So think about the promotion while you're studying hard for it, and anticipate that six-month beach party once you've successfully completed your finals.

revise comprehensively before your exams? How many times have you decided it would be a great idea to go out with your mates, family or anyone to avoid the nightmare task of knuckling down to your study? But all the delay does is to make an already tough job ten times worse. Now why on earth would you want to do that? Are you some kind of masochist? All this means that you will probably spend more time avoiding doing your study and revision than you would have spent doing it. Of course, when you are making these decisions you don't think of the future pain – all you want to do is avoid the current pain you associate with study.

Key to changing this is to change the unconscious behaviours we have built up over the years. And the good news is that we can.

Our brains are powerful instruments, and just as we can learn a new skill and subject, so we can unlearn bad habits and behaviours and replace them with new ones. If you do a sport, you probably do this all the time. For example, a coach will point out a bad habit to you, say on your serve when playing tennis. She will also tell you how to serve correctly. Armed with this new knowledge, you will practise the new technique until your serve is perfect. It's the same way with our studying behaviours.

The way to switch our behaviours is to ask a series of questions which the guys from Catalyst (Jim Steele, Colin Hiles and Martin Coburn) use on their neuro-linguistic programming (NPL) courses. This questioning approach is designed to make us recognise that avoiding short-term pain only serves to

Why do people insist on analysing their performance as soon as they've finished an exam? They shouldn't, and IDEA 50, *Leave the scalpel behind*, will tell you why.

Try another idea...

generate long-term pain. In other words, the pain is unavoidable, and the longer you leave it the worse it can become (and don't we know it?). Common sense really, but many of us don't follow it. Here are the questions:

Pain

■ What would happen if I took no action at all (i.e. not study or revise)?

■ What would be the costs of taking no action (such as time, problems later on and so on)?

■ What pain would it cause me?

■ How would it make me feel right now (projecting the pain of the future into the present)?

Pleasure

■ What would happen if I took action now (i.e. complete my study and revise)?

'The aim of the wise is not to secure pleasure, but to avoid pain.'
ARISTOTLE

Defining idea...

■ What would be the benefits?

■ What pleasure would it give me?

- How would it make me feel right now (projecting the pleasure of the future into the present)?

Give it a try and I can guarantee that it won't be long before you are focused and dedicated to completing your study and preparing for your exams in plenty of time.

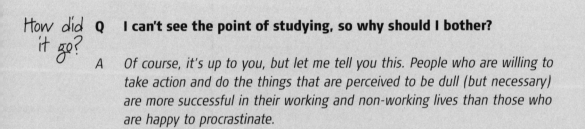

How did it go?

Q **I can't see the point of studying, so why should I bother?**

A *Of course, it's up to you, but let me tell you this. People who are willing to take action and do the things that are perceived to be dull (but necessary) are more successful in their working and non-working lives than those who are happy to procrastinate.*

Q **How on earth can you turn pain into pleasure – especially with study?**

A *It's simple, really. Think about the consequences of not studying or revising: increased stress and worry about not being fully prepared; the likelihood that you will fail your exams; the disappointment that follows; the pressure to retake them, which means you have to do all the work again; the impact of the failure on your academic career and your chance of a good job. Sounds pretty depressing, doesn't it? Now think about the consequences of studying and preparing for your exams when you should: you will probably pass; you will feel good that you have succeeded; you won't have to retake; you will be able to tackle higher qualifications and you could secure a good job. Now, that's much better isn't it?*

32

Are you receiving me?

Oral exams are an important part of the exam system and are frequently used for vocational courses and professional exams. They test other skills than written tests, such as your ability to communicate and think on your feet.

Standing in front of a panel of people who are there to grill you is many people's idea of a nightmare. Keeping your cool and not getting tongue-tied is just as important as knowing your stuff. Can you handle it?

Most of us will take an oral exam at some point in our studying career. Whether it is spoken English, French or German, a viva at university or a professional interview, orals are a popular way to test how well you are able to articulate your knowledge. The real difference between the written and oral exam is that the examiner will ask you questions that you cannot fully prepare for because you will not have had the questions before hand, and then you will be taken down a line of questioning by the examiner based upon your answers. With so many options, it is impossible to prepare for specific questions. So it is certainly less straightforward than the written

Here's an idea for you... If you find yourself facing an oral exam, enlist the help of a friend. Get her to take on the role of the examiner so that you can get used to having someone listening to your every word. She can also give you feedback on how well you come across. To add some fun, ask her to score you on star quality. Videoing your performance can be even more helpful. You might find watching yourself uncomfortable, but it will give a warts-and-all idea of how you come across. The more polished and confident you are, the higher the marks you'll get, so overcome that self-consciousness and give it a go.

exam, where you are only asked one question and if you are well prepared can have the complete answer to hand. Most oral examiners will attempt to test the limits of your knowledge, and this is particularly the case in the university viva and professional interviews. You therefore have to be even more prepared than if you were taking a written paper, so you could probably do with some hints and tips for your preparation. First, it is a good idea to find out what you will be examined on. For language orals you are usually expected to read some text out loud (which you may have seen previously) and converse in the language under examination. In other cases you will be provided with a brief or will be expected to discuss a project, your dissertation or your professional experience in some detail. In this instance, the examiners will have studied a copy of your project or professional record before you turn up. On some courses you will be expected to prepare and give a presentation, which can be a daunting prospect for those of us who are not used to it. If you don't get a brief, ask for one, and it is always a good idea to ask your tutor to provide you with a few practice questions and then critique you on your response. You can always do the same with your fellow students who are also going through the same experience.

When you are in the exam make sure you are polite throughout and remember that it usually starts the minute you walk through the door, so be on your toes, smile, maintain eye contact with the examiner(s) and give them all your attention. Yes, it will be stressful, but remember who's in charge here and behave accordingly, as examiners are more likely to be lenient if you build up a good rapport with them. Try to remain as calm as possible by taking deep breaths and not rushing into questions. Although pauses will seem like a very long time to you, they won't to the examiner, so don't be afraid to use them. Pauses are necessary in order to give you time to think and construct your answer; rushing usually leads to mistakes. If you don't understand a question, ask the examiner to either repeat it or reword it for you, and if you don't know the answer, come clean and tell them. It is always a better approach – you can't ramble your way out like you can in a written paper. Try to avoid simple yes or no answers by providing a balanced argument or examples from your knowledge of the subject. When the exam is finished, thank the examiner for his time and leave.

Finally, when you have finished, relax for a while, as orals are more stressful than written exams and a lot more exhausting.

Try another idea...

Learning how to think positively is one of the most important things you can do to boost both your studies and your results. So if you reckon you could do with a boost, take a peek at IDEA 19, *The power of positive thinking*.

Defining idea...

'Grasp the subject, the words will follow.'
CATO THE ELDER

How did
it go?

Q **Thanks for the tips. Are there any other ways I could improve my chances?**

A *Getting involved with public debates, giving presentations of any kind and performing recitals are all ways to practise public speaking and should make the oral exam a little easier to cope with. Another thing you can do is to record yourself and play it back to assess your performance, or just practise speaking out loud. (Try not to do this late at night or you'll wake the neighbours and don't do it on the bus unless you don't mind the stares!)*

Q **I heard that you need good listening skills. Is this true?**

A *Yes, it is. In fact, it's possibly one of the most important skills you need for an oral exam. Listening to the questions being asked of you instead of trying to second guess them or loading up with your answer before they have finished is crucial. The more attentive you are at listening the better your answers should be.*

Q **What if I make a mistake?**

A *If you make a mistake just let them know; don't try and blunder your way out as the examiners will spot this a mile off. And remember, each question is new, so you can put the bad one behind you and start afresh with the next. Most mistakes can be put down to a combination of nerves and poor listening skills.*

33

Breaking the four-minute mile

How do you prepare for your exams? Do you pace up and down? Feverishly smoke cigarettes? Or are you one of the few calm people floating around on a sea of serenity? With visualisation, you could be.

Before an exam I'd be just like a caged lion, snarling at my fellow students and pacing up and down until it was time to enter the exam hall. I didn't want to speak to anyone; I just wanted to get it over and done with.

Before Roger Bannister broke the four-minute mile, conventional wisdom (especially from the medical profession) believed that it was impossible. Indeed, doctors at the time thought that anyone who attempted it would die. Bannister believed it was possible though, despite the fact that there were no models on which to base his belief. So how did he do it? Well, he rehearsed the race over and over again in his mind, feeling, seeing and sensing everything that would happen

143

Here's an idea for you...

When preparing for your exam set yourself some questions to answer. To begin with, capture the key points you want to make on cue cards. Rehearse these out loud (where you can't be disturbed) until you feel confident enough to remember them without referring to your notes. If you do this for all the main questions you could be asked, you will come across as someone who knows their stuff.

through the ideal race in full Technicolor. When the day came he had the race fully mapped out and all he had to do was run it in real-time. The rest, as they say, is history. Of course, as soon as this new benchmark had been achieved a clutch of athletes did exactly the same.

So what does this mean for those of us faced with an exam? Well, it requires us to apply the same visualisation techniques which Bannister used then and all modern athletes apply now. And this means that we have to change our attitude, not develop some kind of superhuman abilities. So the good news is that it's in everyone's reach. So just as Bannister was able to practise running the race of his life, so you can do exactly the same by practising sitting and successfully completing your exams in your very own imaginary exam hall! You can paint it how you like and even make the invigilator look like a clown if that helps!

Sit down in a quiet room and mentally take yourself to your exam. Imagine yourself walking into the hall, settling down, placing your pens, calculator and other equipment neatly on your desk. Sense how you feel as you look around the room and wait for the 'Please open your papers now'. As you read the questions, sense how your confidence rises as you recall all the information you have learnt and watch yourself as you complete each question perfectly. As you visualise the questions, work out how you will approach them, and as you complete them keep an eye on the imaginary clock in the exam hall to ensure you finish the paper in plenty of time. Do this once a day starting a few weeks before the exam and you will feel more confident as a result.

Attitude is critical to you successfully completing your studies. Most of us don't give it much thought, but there are some advantages if we do, as IDEA 3, *It's all about attitude, dude*, explains.

Try another idea...

The technique of visualisation is borrowed from neuro-linguistic programming (NLP), which was derived from research into the transference of therapy skills between counsellors. The N component of NLP states that our behaviour stems from the way we experience the world around us through our five senses (see, hear, feel, touch and taste). It also relates to our physiological reactions to the things we sense. The L component relates to the language we use to order our thoughts and behaviour, as well as the language we use to communicate with those around us. Finally, the P aspect refers to the way we choose to respond to conditions around us. There are two elements to NLP which are particularly relevant to studying. The first is understanding and changing our belief systems so that we can become more effective at studying and taking exams, and the second is how we maintain our peak performance and high mental state required for the exams themselves. So the next time you are worrying about your exams, take some time out and visualise yourself completing them successfully. You will become supremely confident and everyone will wonder what you are on.

'Whether you think you can or whether you think you can't, you're probably right.'
HENRY FORD

Defining idea...

How did it go?

Q   I am struggling with this visualisation thing. Will it ever work?

A   *The key is to go with the flow. It might feel alien to begin with, but over time you will get used to it. The thing to remember is that your brain finds it impossible to distinguish between imagination and reality. So if you were to imagine that you were sucking a lemon, the effect would be the same as if you really were (except, perhaps, for the scurvy). All you need is a good imagination.*

Q   Should I visualise only good outcomes?

A   *Although this might feel a little uncomfortable, it is a good idea to use the same visualisation technique to run through some of the more difficult aspects of the exam, like finding you can't answer all the questions, or you fail to turn up in time. Then, using the same technique, you can work out your strategies for remaining calm and dealing with the issue in hand. On the day of the exam you should feel doubly confident in your ability to handle any situation.*

Q   Should I use it on the day?

A   *You shouldn't need to. Having spent time visualising a successful outcome in the exam, when it comes to the day itself it should go like clockwork. If you find yourself panicking though, you might just briefly visualise success so as to steady yourself before focusing back on the task in hand. If you have worked on the technique long enough you will find that its effects are dramatic and you will feel much calmer as a result.*

34

Dreaming of dissertations

You can't escape the final project, dissertation or report, and if you prepare it well it can mean the difference between an average grade and an excellent one.

Reports and dissertations test more than just your ability to recall facts and figures: there's original thought and research involved too. I think they're a lot more interesting than sitting exams. They are certainly less stressful.

No matter what kind of studying you are doing, be it pre-university, university or professional/vocational, there is an increasing requirement to complete a written project of some kind or other. These can take one of many forms, including those listed below. Sometimes they are defined by your tutor or the course you are following, and sometimes you have control over what approach you wish to adopt. The important thing to remember is that each type of project will require a slightly different approach in its completion. The main types are:

- *Surveys.* Here you are sampling using questionnaires and/or interviews in order to collect information which you can then draw conclusions from or come up with insights about. The principal skill to apply here is the ability to structure

Make sure you cover all the bases for your project by using a checklist. Incorporate the following features:

- **objectives (and agree with your tutor)**
- **scope (number of words, approach, etc.)**
- **title (and agree with your tutor)**
- **literature review**
- **frameworks and models which could be used**
- **methodology (questionnaire, interviews, case studies, etc.)**
- **structure of report (introduction, objectives, methods, results, analysis/ discussion, conclusions, recommendations, bibliography)**

Run the draft by your tutor prior to finalising and handing in.

the questionnaires/interviews so that they are able to answer the objective you posed for the project. Of all the possible types of project, this may appear to be the simplest, but is often the hardest. One of the most difficult things is to ensure you get enough responses to be able to draw useful conclusions.

- *Research.* This involves investigating a particular topic in some detail. It might be a literature review, which requires you to capture and critique what other people have written about a subject, or it might involve you using the available literature to inform your own ideas or theories. In this instance, the examiners will be looking for some original thought and how the existing thinking supports or counters your argument.

- *Case studies.* These are in-depth analyses of particular companies, initiatives (such as major IT projects) or concepts (such as a particular management theory). Their purpose is to draw out some specific conclusions and learning points from a real-life example which can be tested against a model or framework. Selecting the right case study is critical to this type of project, as it should be rich enough for you to come up with some meaty conclusions. Case studies are increasingly used within job interviews (especially consultancy), so this type of project could be beneficial in other ways too. (Two birds, one stone: I'm sure you can work it out.)

Completing a project on your own is not the only time when you are expected to put original ideas to paper: there's also the group project. To make yours great fun rather than a complete nightmare, see IDEA 9, *Too many cooks?*.

Try another idea...

- *The professional critique.* In many professions, there is a requirement to prepare a report based upon some post-qualification work experience. Such reports often take place after 2–3 years of employment and are designed to test your knowledge of a particular subject. You are normally free to select the topic, although in some instances you have to check it out with the professional body you wish to join to see if it is acceptable. Having chosen the topic, you are expected to write up the project/experience and then analyse it. Once complete, you submit your critique for assessment and if it's okay, you are admitted to the profession.

I remember sitting in my tutor's office a couple of years ago discussing a topic I had selected for a report I had to write. There I was, all excited, saying 'how about something on geographical information systems?' As Steve (the tutor) sat there, puffing away at his pipe, I could see that

'The quality of a man's life is in direct proportion to his commitment to excellence, regardless of his chosen field of endeavor.'
VINCE LOMBARDI

Defining idea...

he wasn't too happy with the idea. I asked him what else was on his mind and he suggested another topic, which was even more interesting. Very often, tutors know best, and asking for their input when you have drawn a blank is a great idea because, like the tower in Pisa, they always have a list.

149

How did
it go? **Q Do I need to come up with something earth-shatteringly new for my project?**

A   *The simple answer is no. There is no requirement for you to solve world hunger or the energy crisis. And tutors don't expect you to either. If it was that simple, they'd probably already have done it. Of course, if you do so along the way, then that's great. The whole point of completing a project is to test your ability to undertake some research and, more importantly, your skill at managing the whole process on your own.*

Q How do I select the subject?

A   *As there is a lot of personal choice involved with this, I recommend you make a list of topics which you find interesting. This may be the first time you have been given some choice in your studying career, and the best way to maintain motivation is to choose something that sparks your interest. Naturally, you will need to confirm your selection with your tutor, which I'm sure will be fine.*

Q How should I approach it?

A   *Follow the general approach I've suggested and you won't go far wrong. In the end, if you plan the project thoroughly, check it out with your tutor and then stick to it, you should be in a good position to earn a very good mark.*

35

The dark side

Although it might masquerade as a cunning plan, cheating is in fact a bad idea; well, it is if you get caught. Whether you are up against it, lazy or just downright devious, cheating is no substitute for good exam technique.

In a remote north-eastern state in India, separatist rebels shot a number of people they suspected of helping students cheat in exams. Elsewhere, a bunch of students set fire to the chief of a veterinary college because he refused to let them cheat. Cheating is a serious business!

These days, every student and tutor is under pressure to perform. From league tables to first-class honours, high grades are an entry point to a glittering academic or commercial career. They are also one of the best ways an institution can get increased funding, more money for the teachers and research cash from commerce. So it's no surprise everyone is at it: cheating, that is. In some instances teachers and lecturers have written their students' essays in order to get a greater number through the system. There was even a case of an American student paying another

Here's an idea for you...

If you ever feel tempted to cheat, take time out to write down a list of the consequences. When compiling this list don't just think about the immediate consequences, but think about the impact on your future academic and working careers – and the long-term guilt. Hopefully this will stop you from trying it on.

girl to take a three-year degree course for her. Of course there will always be cheats, but these days the sophistication of the available technology and the increasing use of coursework to assess candidates provides ample opportunity for the conniving student to bend the rules a bit. So what are the common ways students cheat? For those of you who are curious, purely for academic reasons of course, here they are:

- Writing on your body. A bit low tech these days, but still popular. From the back of your hand to the length of your arm, any piece of flesh that can be made visible is fair game.

- Writing on the desk. This is a bit tricky unless you know the actual desk you will be sitting at and, of course, have the opportunity to sneak in and jot down some key notes beforehand without being spotted. Either that or you'll have to write on all the desks!

- Mobile phones and concealed microphones. This involves the cunning use of hidden devices which allow the student to talk to their friend who is outside of the exam hall with a pile of notes. Once the question has been relayed, the buddy searches the notes and reads the key elements of the question back to the cheat.

■ Paying someone to write essays for you. A common and highly effective approach, apart from one simple drawback: the style is usually very different and the essay sticks out like a sore thumb. More sophisticated approaches involve the student supplying a recent essay so that the ghost writer can match their style more precisely.

Maybe you cheat because you hate studying and especially exams. If so, then take a look at IDEA 31, *No gain without pain*.

Try another idea...

■ Downloading essays and other coursework assignments from the internet. A simple approach, but also simple to detect with the sophisticated software available to teachers these days. And teacher is just as capable of searching the internet as you are.

■ Having a buddy hold up his or her answer sheet so that you can read the answers. Not a great one this, as they would have to be holding it up for so long for you to copy it all down that even a sleeping invigilator would spot it. And have you seen the state of people's handwriting in exams?

■ Stealing the exam papers themselves. This has been known to occur every once in a while but usually ends up in failure as once the theft has been uncovered the examination board cancels the exam and everyone has to sit a new one. Not very popular with your fellow students.

■ Bribing the teacher or examiner. A bit of a long shot, but desperate times call for desperate measures.

'A smart person knows all the rules so he can break them wisely.'
LUBNA AZMI

Defining idea...

In the end, of course, cheating is for fools, because by the time you have read the smudged notes on your arm or spent ages trying to catch what your friend is telling you down the microphone, you could have written at least two essays. You may get some marks, but you'll never get the elusive A grade because cheating just takes too long. Not only that, it can be very expensive to boot. You are far better off relying on that powerful thing between your ears – yes, your brain.

How did it go?

Q   So what you are saying is that I shouldn't cheat, right?

A   *Yep. If you are well prepared there should be no need. Plus these days the ability to detect whether someone has cheated is just as easy as cheating itself. If you are tempted to cheat, just think about the consequences.*

Q   But, if I was really tempted, which approach should I adopt?

A   *Nice try, but you're going to have to get your help somewhere else, I'm afraid. Plus if you do try, the likelihood of you getting away with it is pretty slim, and I try not to mix with losers. Now go back to your revision whilst you've still got time.*

36

Stacking the shelves

How good are you at recalling all the information you need in an exam? If you find it tricky, which most of us do, you might want to use the techniques outlined here.

A few years ago I was on course where we were shown a learning technique called the memory stack. We linked 20 key words to detailed concepts. By recalling the words I was able to remember all the detailed stuff. Fantastic!

The encoding of data and information within our brains is highly complex. If you think about it, I'll bet you can remember single images, smells, words and noises which can evoke rich memories. For example, music is one of the most powerful mechanisms for reminding ourselves of events that took place decades ago. Indeed, most of us look back fondly on the music we used to listen to when we were 17–21 and whenever we hear it, it takes us right back. In fact, we can take it further: after hearing just one or two chords you can often remember the whole song, which can bring back the whole era, and so forth. So just imagine if we could do this with our study. Well, actually we can – just so long as we master a few simple techniques that exploit the way our brain functions. The technical name for such memory tools is mnemonics. Here are three which you might find helpful:

Here's an idea for you...

The next time you are in your car use familiar landmarks (pubs, buildings, road junctions and so on) to create a story. The purpose of this is to get you confident in the application of the concept before you apply it to your study, so your story can be anything you like. Once you have finished your journey, try and remember the landmarks and the story together. After a couple of days, repeat the journey and see if the landmarks bring the story back to life. If it works, then give it a try with your study material.

■ Creating a story. Here you need to take out key words from your notes and weave them into a memorable story by linking each one in turn. The story should include all your key words and can be as colourful as you like. In fact, the more colourful it is the more likely it is that you'll remember it.

■ Going on a journey using key landmarks as the verbal/visual cues you need to recall your notes. This is very similar to the story approach, but here you are going on a familiar journey that you might take every day, such as going to school, college or work. As you follow the journey you should associate your key facts and information with landmarks along the way, like sign posts, road junctions and roundabouts, key buildings and so on.

■ Using a peg system, through which you link your facts and figures to specific words, number sequences or the alphabet. As these sequences are standard, the art is in how you associate the number, letter or word with the information you need to recall. The real beauty of this approach is that the sequence is preset (i.e. 1, 2, 3..., 10; a, b, c..., z).

In order to make these techniques work for you I recommend that you do the following. From your notes create a series of learning points; those things which you believe are vital to the subject you are studying. The learning points will act as gateways to the detail which you will need to recall in the exam. Then use a single word, or number if you prefer, to create an association with each of the learning points. If you are using words, the word should have some relation to the learning point you are trying to remember. Draw up a table or list, with the key words on one side and the corresponding learning points on the other. Then develop a simple story around the key words so that you can link them together. Once developed, walk through the story in your head (or out loud if you prefer) and repeat it a few times. If you are using numbers you just have to make sure you remember which learning point goes with which number, which, if you are mathematically inclined, could be easier than creating a story.

Developing all your revision aids from scratch is as pointless as reinventing the wheel – why make your own when there are plenty to go round? There are a lot of study aids out there, and IDEA 8, *Standing on the shoulders of giants*, will tell you all about them.

Try another idea...

Like most other study techniques, mnemonics will create and then reinforce the synaptic links between the individual neurons within your brain. The strength of these synaptic links depends on how often the neurons fire across them. Therefore, the more the story or mind stack is repeated, the stronger the synapses will become and the easier it will be to call up the information. Most of us can recite our times

'Your memory is a monster; you forget it remembers. It simply files things away. It keeps things from you, or hides things from you and summons them for you to recall with a will of its own. You think you have memory; but it has you!'
JOHN IRVING

Defining idea...

tables even though we learnt them a long time ago as young children. It was the constant repetition of 'one times one is one, two times one is two' and so on that created the very strong synaptic links which means we can now recall the information effortlessly. What I am recommending here is that you do the same sort of thing for your wider studies.

How did it go?

Q This sounds great, but does it really work?

A Yes! The use of memory stacks and other mnemonics is a well-known technique and will improve your memory. And, like any system, the more times you use it the more effective it will become. Don't fall into the trap of trying it once, failing and then giving up. Perseverance is the key to success here.

Q Which approach should I use?

A Quite simply, the one that you feel most comfortable with. If you are more into lists, then using the peg system might be more effective. Alternatively, if you like to tell stories, then the story or journey approach might be better. The best thing to do is try a couple out and see which serves you the best.

37

Don't panic!

Two words link Douglas Adams's book *The Hitch Hiker's Guide to the Galaxy* and the British TV institution, *Dad's Army*. 'Don't Panic' should be inscribed onto every student's forehead.

Stress seems to go hand in hand with exams and studying. No matter what the level, or how trivial the exam, we all get a little stressed. A little stress is a good thing, because it keeps you alert. It's when it builds up that the problems start.

One of the questions I was asked when I applied to university was whether I got anxious during exams. My response was a big yes, as at that time I used to get very worked up about them. To my surprise, they put me on the top floor of the hall of residence I was assigned to. Then, as I started to make friends, I found that all the worriers had been given rooms on the top floor! Did they want us to jump or something? Top floor aside, it is important to be able to get to grips with stress and manage it if you are going to get the most out of your studying and your exams. Being able to manage your stress levels involves three steps. First, you must

Here's an idea for you...

Ask your fellow students about what makes them stressed and how they cope with it. There are three main advantages of doing this: first, you'll see that it's not only you who gets stressed; secondly, you could get some useful ideas on how to best manage it; and finally, you'll have created a support network of friends who can all support each other...great!

recognise the signs of stress, which can include rapid breathing, hot flushes, the feeling of butterflies in your stomach, stomach cramps, biting your nails, problems getting to sleep and staying asleep, irritability and a desire to unwind with drink and cigarettes...the list is almost endless! Once you recognise the signs, you need to identify the triggers that cause the anxiety. This can be done by taking a few minutes to gather your thoughts and then listing down all of the causes of stress in your life and especially study. The final step is taking action to either eliminate or reduce those causes, or if this is impossible, building in coping mechanisms to reduce the levels of stress when you experience the triggers. Some of the things that people have advised me to do in the past include:

■ Be as prepared as possible. There is no doubt that the more prepared you are, the less stress you should feel. So apart from feeling a little apprehensiveness as you open the exam paper, that should be it.

■ Seek input from your tutor, who will be able to provide you with some one-to-one advice. Tutors will have seen plenty of stressed students over the years and will probably have a whole raft of advice, hints and tips that you could use. They could also bolster your self-confidence by telling you that you are not actually a hopeless case after all.

■ Make good use of your time through effective time management and prioritisation. In other words, make a revision timetable and stick to it. In this way you can maintain a clear focus on work but not overdo it.

- Try not to compare yourself with other students, especially the very clever ones! Some students are naturals who will always get the highest grades. The best person to compete against is yourself.

If you find things don't work out and your results are worse than you expected, then take some solace in IDEA 52, *Don't worry, be happy.*

Try another idea...

- Take sufficient breaks during your study periods to ensure you don't become too obsessive about the task in hand. Remember, if you start early enough you won't need to worry about taking breaks (another source of stress, if ever there was one).

- Undertake regular physical activity, be it your favourite sport (I do fencing and English martial arts), walking, swimming or jogging. It's easy to lock yourself away and just study, but it's also important to understand the benefits of exercise on your physiology and particularly how you feel.

- Get plenty of sleep, ideally around eight hours a night.

- Maintain a healthy diet, so out with the junk food and in with fish, vegetables and fruit.

- Improve your breathing technique so that you inhale and exhale more deeply – this oxygenates your blood and makes you more able to deal with the problem that is causing you to become stressed.

'If you can't sleep, then get up and do something instead of lying there worrying. It's the worry that gets you, not the lack of sleep.'
DALE CARNEGIE

Defining idea...

- Take up yoga or other relaxation technique, like Tai Chi. I do yoga: it's great, if a little painful!

Most schools, colleges and universities offer confidential help lines and counselling to support those students who get particularly stressed. The thing to remember about this type of support is that it is there for a very good reason and you have every right to use it. The very process of talking your problems through with someone will alleviate, if not remove, the symptoms of anxiety. Better out than in!

Q   What should I do if I get stressed out in the exam?

A   *The best thing to do is to stop what you are doing temporarily, shut your eyes and take some deep breaths. At the same time you should think positive thoughts, so that when you reopen your eyes you will have pushed aside all those negative thoughts that stressed you out. This process will open up your brain (the reasoning part of which, the cortex, would have shut down when you were stressed – don't worry, it's designed to do that) and help you get over the problem.*

Q   If it is really bad, what else can I do?

A   *You could always try hypnosis. I have known very stressed students who have gone to a hynotherapist and have come back raring to go. What's more they looked supremely confident in the exam hall. Needless to say, they passed. If you are going to go in for hypnotherapy, make sure you do it in advance of the exam – hypnotherapists aren't usually allowed into exam halls, not even for open book exams.*

38

Exam hall excellence

When those magic words 'You may now turn over your exam paper' punctuate the silence of the exam hall, it's time to put your exam hall skills to the test.

I'm sure you've been there: head down, spewing out everything you know about your favourite topic. You know it all, you're on a roll, you glance at the clock — and half the time is gone and you're still on question 1!

One of the simplest ways to reduce the amount of marks you pick up in any exam is to answer too few questions. Even when faced with situations where you can't answer all the questions (maybe because you have focused your revision too narrowly, or just not put enough effort in), you are still better off attempting the required number of questions, as you will still pick up marks no matter how feeble your effort. It always used to amaze me when students would walk out of the exam hall halfway through the exam. I used to think that they must be very good or very stupid; it was inevitably the latter, because they all failed. Avoiding some of their pitfalls is easy, but how to ensure you answer all the questions you need to in the time allotted? Here's how.

Here's an idea for you...

You pick up the majority of your marks in the first half of the essay, so practise building structures to your answers that bring in as much as possible into this critical first half. Once you get beyond halfway, you are entering into the world of diminishing returns. If you can condition yourself in this way, you will pick up a good score even if you begin to run out of time.

■ As you read the question, underline the key words and phrases to ensure that you know where to focus all the material that is inevitably flooding into your head.

■ Once you have read the question, spend a few minutes writing the plan. The plan should outline (to yourself and the examiner) how you intend to answer the question and what material you need to introduce, and allows you to recall and note all the major dates, key facts and bullets you want to build into the essay. Don't be tempted to skip this because you consider it a waste of time: a little planning now can save you many minutes of scribbling aimlessly in a disjointed flow of consciousness that is more likely to lose you marks for incoherence.

■ Don't be tempted to write down everything you know about the topic. The examiner is not looking for a brain dump. Targeting your examples, facts and figures to the question will allow you to improve your overall marks. This is why it is so critical to both read the question *and* plan the answer.

■ Keep a mental note of how much time you have for each answer and how much time you have allotted to complete each component of the answer. For example, you could give yourself 5 minutes to plan the response, 45 minutes to answer it and then 10 minutes to have a quick read through to make sure that your dates, facts, figures and assertions are correct. This should help to minimise the number of silly errors which creep in when you are under pressure.

If you want to know how to pick up the maximum score, it's a good idea to know how marks are allocated. See IDEA 6, *On your marks.*

Try another idea...

- Make sure you have a watch to hand to ensure that you keep to time. Keep a frequent eye on it to prevent you from overrunning. If you do start to overrun, set a clear cut off time when you will complete the answer in summary form.

- Always focus on a great introduction and conclusion. In particular, make sure the conclusion has a high impact, as this will create the impression that you are someone who knows your subject.

Despite taking all the measures outlined above, it still pays to have a safety net just in case. The best way to do this is to answer the questions in the right order. You should always start with the one you are most confident with, then work through the rest in descending order of confidence. As long as you keep to the allotted number of minutes in the first one, you should leave yourself sufficient time to tackle the other questions. You have to resist the temptation to spend too much time on your favourite topic, and you shouldn't tackle the most difficult question first because this eats up precious time with limited return.

'*I recommend to you to take care of minutes: for hours will take care of themselves.*'
LORD CHESTERFIELD

Defining idea...

How did it go?

Q   What if I start to run out of time? What should I do?

A   *First it will help if you have made a rough plan of the essay before you start, as the examiners will turn to this to see what you would have written about and may even award a mark or two for it. A better approach is to list out the key facts, figures and arguments in bulleted form at the end of the essay (in essence, where you realised you were running out of time). Although there is no real structure to these, it is likely that you will pick up some additional marks because you have at least noted the salient points.*

Q   Do you recommend that I read the answers?

A   *I have to admit that I hate checking my answers, especially if they are essay based. I do think it's a good idea to check for gross errors, such as wrong dates, but I don't favour rereading the whole thing. My view is that if you have allotted your time correctly there is no time to rewrite it if it is wrong. So publish and be damned, that's what I suggest. You may not agree with this, but just think how you'll feel if you read through it all, want to rewrite it but realise you haven't got the time. Why put yourself through it? So I recommend a rapid pass looking for the howlers.*

39

Learning how to learn

We tend to muddle through when it comes to learning. We sit in lectures and listen intently, make notes and then do our best to regurgitate them in the exam. Surely there must be a better way?

There has been a lot of research into the process through which we learn. Which is great, as it helps us mere mortals get to grips with our own learning process, which is no bad thing.

As a very young child, learning was an effortless experience. Each and every one of us would absorb and assimilate vast amounts of information at an amazing rate. Now I find it a struggle remembering today's date! Now that might be my age, but it's a common theme. Studying requires us to hoover up vast amounts of information which we hope we will retain and actually learn something from. Most of us do it in a haphazard way, without any real thought about how the process works, so I thought it would be a great idea to tell you.

Here's an idea for you...

Ask your tutor to provide some feedback on your learning style. In particular, ask them to identify your strengths (e.g. ability to ask questions, comprehend subjects and write essays) and where you could improve. Such feedback will be invaluable when it comes to designing your study.

As you learn something new, the neurons within the frontal cortex become busy and so do many of their neighbours. This spreading out of brain activity is necessary to cope with the volume of input during the learning process. Once the neurons have fired together more than once, the cells and synapses between them change chemically so that when one neuron fires again it will be a stronger trigger to the other. This is called Hebbian learning (after Donald Hebb, who discovered it). The amount of energy used during the learning process is considerable, which helps explain why we feel so tired when learning something new. The really interesting thing about the brain and the learning process is that, with enough practice, the skills you learn become hard wired. Hard wiring in this instance involves the information you have learnt passing from the higher cortex to the subcortical area of the brain. And this is important because it releases the neurons associated with learning in the cortex to learn new things.

One model of learning I find especially helpful is the Kolb model. This model is probably the most widely known tool for describing the learning process and determining an individual's learning preferences. By assessing your learning style, you can formulate learning experiences that allow you to get the most out of the process of study. According to Kolb, the process of learning follows four steps that form a continuous, never-ending cycle:

Step 1 – *Concrete experience.* As this suggests, it's learning from experience.

Step 2 – *Reflective observation.* This involves reflecting on events (which we experienced in Step 1), considering alternative courses of action and seeking out the meaning of things.

Step 3 – *Abstract conceptualisation.* This involves the formulation of abstract concepts and generalisations through the logical analysis which comes through Step 2.

Step 4 – *Active experimentation.* This involves testing the implications of new concepts through deliberate action.

There are four types of learners, corresponding to each of the four stages:

- Activists (which corresponds to concrete experience) – these are people who prefer to act rather than think in the learning process. Such people prefer to rely on intuition rather than logic and prefer to learn in a real world setting rather than the classroom. Trial and error is their primary method of learning.

Another way of looking at the learning process, which relates to our sensory preferences, is presented in IDEA 44, *See, hear, feel.*

Try another idea...

'You can have the best imagination in the world with the brainpower of several Einsteins, but if you don't feed it, it will wither and die. And the great thing about feeding the brain is that it doesn't get fat and flabby and slow. It has a near infinite capacity for information.'
MARC LEWIS

Defining idea...

■ Reflectors (which corresponds to reflection and observation) – these are people who prefer to consider the pros and cons of things. They like to take a lot of points of view and information on board before taking action. Such people prefer to learn through observation and from other people. Time is the biggest issue for the reflector, as they need plenty of it to achieve what they need.

■ Theorists (which corresponds to abstract conceptualisation) – these people learn through abstract thinking and modelling, rather than taking action. Theorists prefer to conduct research as part of the learning process.

■ Pragmatists (which corresponds to active experimentation) – these people learn best by tackling a practical problem. They prefer to be given hints, tips and practical steps to success rather than researching it for themselves. They generally accept received wisdom without question.

Q **So how do I get my brain used to learning, then?**

How did it go?

A *There are a few things you could try. In fact, experts recommend that you do a combination of things. You can use puzzles to help strengthen your spatial skills. You can write to enhance your language abilities. You can debate to develop your reasoning capabilities. And you can network with intelligent and interesting people to enhance the general connectivity within the brain.*

Q **Does that mean I can be good at everything – like an A-grade student?**

A *Possibly. Sure, there are those students who are gifted and will always get top grades. But many of these people also work incredibly hard to achieve the grades they want, and maybe you don't. We all have the mental capacity to be good at everything, but there is more than just one form of intelligence, so you can't expect to be brilliant at everything.*

Q **So what are these other intelligences, then, and can I see which ones I'm good at?**

A *According to psychologist Howard Gardner, we all have a mix of nine intelligences. These are linguistic (information in verbal and written form), mathematical/technical (description, instructions and logical thinking), visual (pictures), auditory (sound and music), kinaesthetic/motor (ability to understand complex machinery and mechanics), interpersonal (what is now called emotional intelligence), intrapersonal (how good you are at knowing yourself), naturalistic (no not naturism) and philosophical/ethical (ability to read situations). There are tests you can take and these can be insightful.*

171

40

More can be more

For those amongst you who have to study maths, and especially the complex stuff, there is one important thing to remember – show your working out, as this is the only way to maximise your marks.

Watching a lecturer scribble line after line of complex stuff on two blackboards was not the best way for me to learn maths. Throwing paper darts at him, though much more fun, was not much of an improvement. Fortunately I found the way.

There are important differences between studying something like English or history and studying maths. In the non-mathematical subjects you are not dealing with truths, so you are always able to debate a subject using different opinions. In maths, however, there is only one correct answer. This means that you have to focus much more on how the answer is derived than the answer itself. It also means that you will have to pay a little more attention than perhaps I did when I was throwing paper darts, although one did drift gracefully to the front of the lecture theatre and came in to land on the desk in front of the lecturer to a round of applause! When it

Here's an idea for you...

If, like me, you find understanding maths a struggle, get round the need to understand by learning the derivation or solution to a problem by rote. The way to do this is to write down the perfect solution and learn it. Write it out and check it over and over until you know it by heart. So long as your mind doesn't go blank in the exam, you'll pick up marks without needing to think.

comes to taking notes during your maths lessons/lectures, I recommend that you:

- Listen actively, which means writing down the important stuff, and especially how formulae are derived and how they can help you to arrive at the answer.

- Make sure you note down and understand how you get from one step to the next in solving the problem; this will be an important skill when it comes to the exams (more of that in a moment).

- Ask questions if you are unsure. This is the best time to clarify points, as otherwise you will have to take time out of your lecturer's/teacher's busy schedule. You might feel a little silly, but better that than coming across the problem in the middle of the exam and being unable to solve it.

- Make a special note of any important concepts, rules and techniques.

Once you get down to the studying before the exams, I recommend that you use as many sources as possible and practise as much as you can. The one thing about maths is that you need to be able to apply the rules, concepts and techniques to different questions, and it is the application of these that will get you through the exam. I use a combination of textbooks (and not just the ones provided), which often have questions and answers in them, study guides, which contain reminders of the material you covered in your classes, and past papers. Of all subjects, it is maths that requires the most practice (well, it did for me anyway). When practising it is also a good idea to write out the problems from the textbook or revision guide and see if you can solve them yourself. Once you have finished, you can check your result against the model answers. Other tips that you may find helpful include:

There were times when I just found maths too hard. Did I give up? Heck no. I just got myself a hired hand to give me the advice and practice I needed to gain confidence. Shoot back to IDEA 21, *Hired hand*, to find out more.

Try another idea...

- Think of every rule, technique and approach which might be useful in completing the problem. This will help you to develop flexible problem-solving skills and will build your confidence.

- Start backwards by asking yourself what you need to get to the answer.

- Relate the problem to ones you have solved in the past.

- If possible, break the problem down into smaller parts and solve these individually.

When taking the exam, make sure you:

'*Mathematics may be defined as the subject in which we never know what we are talking about, nor whether what we are saying is true.*'
BERTRAND RUSSELL

Defining idea...

- Read the paper thoroughly at least twice and then prioritise the order in which you will answer the questions. The best way to do this is by gauging how easy each question is to answer and how many marks you'll get for it.

175

■ Show as many workings out as possible, as this will gain you more marks than simply writing down the answer. Even if you know the answer you mustn't skip the steps used to arrive at it – unless, of course, you want to lose marks.

■ Move on if you get stuck. There may be time to come back to the question, but don't dwell.

If you can take all this lot on board, you'll do just fine.

Q   Maths is too difficult. Can't I just give it a miss?

A   *I'm afraid that maths is core to nearly every curriculum these days, and we all need a basic understanding when we go out into the world. If you find it difficult, all I can suggest is that you get as much help as possible. It will pay off.*

Q   Surely solving problems by rote is risky?

A   *It can be, but it's a chance you might have to take on the more tricky aspects. I have done it successfully, although occasionally it can go horribly wrong. I remember learning one derivation, something to do with the shape of the Earth, for my first degree. I had got it off pat. (That's pat, not Pat.) The day of the exam came, I saw the question, got very excited and my mind went blank. I spent the rest of the exam in a blind panic.*

41

Let's get critical

There's one thing that most examiners want to see from candidates and that's critical thinking. Problem is, most us don't even know what it means.

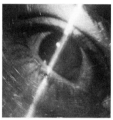

I'm not a great one for accepting any criticism, although I am more than willing to dish it out. But this isn't about being critical for the sake of it; it's about developing some well-honed thinking skills that can improve your studying.

It's funny, isn't it? In the main, it feels as though we spend all our time learning how to record, regurgitate, recognise and paraphrase information. What we don't seem to do is learn how to think critically about what we have learnt and then apply this to open-ended and complex problems. 'So what?' I hear you say. Well, if you were able to develop critical thinking skills you would be more likely to improve your ability to learn and absorb information, and you would almost certainly improve your exam scores. As you'd suspect, questions lie at the heart of

When you are given some reading to do as part of your studying, ask yourself four questions: how much am I going to read? Why am I going to read it (for what purpose)? How am I going to test that I have absorbed what I have read? What study techniques will I use? Use these wisely and you'll build those much sought after critical thinking skills.

critical thinking, and most of us don't ask enough of them. Apart from the usual who, what, why, when, where and how type questions, there is a technique I learnt which will help you develop those questioning skills still further. It is called the fluff buster and is something I picked up on a course a few years ago. The idea is very simple and entails the use of your hands. The left hand is used to capture the most common generalisations we use when speaking and the right hand is used to question their validity. Each finger on the left

Left hand	Right hand
Always	Really always?
Shouldn't, can't, won't, etc.	Who is stopping you from doing x? What if you did x?
Verbs (like to annoy, etc.)	How are they being x (provide examples)?
Non-specific nouns (like they, them etc.)	Who/what is...?
Better, worse, etc.	Compared with what?

hand can be matched to one on the right, so that you can remember the question to ask each time you hear the broad statement. The table shows how this works.

After a while you get used to asking clarifying and hence critical questions when listening to others around you, especially in lectures. And soon you'll be asking your tutor some very tricky questions indeed!

Critical thinking should be applied when you are reading, writing and listening. When reading, you should aim to identify the line of reasoning the author is using and then, once you have identified it, question it by capturing any assumptions and evidence the author has used to support it. Another thing you should do is to evaluate the work against some objective criteria and through this determine whether or not the author's conclusions are supported by what she has written. When writing, you should be able to demonstrate a clear link between the introduction and the conclusion. The conclusions you draw should be based upon the evidence you have included, and you should discuss the point of view from different angles and draw on other writers and sources that allow you to question it. When listening, you should be aiming to check the consistency of the speaker to make sure that what they are saying stacks up and isn't contradictory. If you are really expert, you can watch if his body language is in alignment with what he says.

Everyone recommends that you use active study techniques to get the most out of learning. If you think it's worth investigating, run off to IDEA 23, *Round, round, I get around.*

Try another idea...

'...the quality of our life and that of what we produce, make, or build depends preciously on the quality of our thought.'
MICHAEL SCRIVEN and
RICHARD PAUL, critical thinkers

Defining idea...

You should also be willing to ask questions and challenge them using the fluff-busting questioning technique outlined above.

You know when you have got critical thinking skills when you:

■ Are able to identify and articulate key questions about a subject.

■ Can think openly about a topic and are able to assess whether a point of view (including yours) is valid. In other words, you have balance in your thinking.

■ Are able to reorganise material into categories and understand how it all links together.

■ Can develop your own opinions based upon the facts you have gathered (no more regurgitation for you then).

■ Can test your ideas and conclusions against other information to determine whether they are the best ones.

■ Can communicate complex problems and issues with others and discuss your point of view.

Plato would be proud of you!

Q **Is critical thinking useful beyond studying?**

A *Absolutely. The nature of life, whether it's inside or outside the learning environment, requires us to think critically. Most things have a lot of uncertainty attached to them, so if you can develop good critical thinking skills whilst studying, they'll certainly help you when you have to fend for yourself.*

Q **Are any other models worth using?**

A *I like some of the lateral thinking ideas of Edward De Bono. He is the master of critical thinking, and I especially like his Six Thinking Hats. These hats are designed to separate our thinking into six distinct modes, represented by six coloured 'thinking' hats (white – objective information; red – emotions and feelings; black – logic and negative thoughts; yellow – positive and constructive thoughts; green – creativity and new ideas, and blue – controlling the other hats). The six hats can be great for structuring an essay.*

How did it go?

42

Ever decreasing circles

I bet you've never thought of your study as a circle – well, apart from going round and round in them, of course.

I know people who have very small minds as well as people who have much larger ones (minds, that is). I know who I'd rather spend time with. How about you?

It occurred to me a number of years ago that there is a paradox to learning that runs along the lines of the more you know, the more you don't know. This means that as you develop new skills, learn new capabilities and so on, you realise that rather than mastering a subject, you are only just scraping the surface. There is always much more to learn. In fact, I know people who are accomplished musicians or highly respected experts in their field who believe they know very little. I also know people who are the opposite – they think they know it all but in reality know very little. It occurred to me that I could use a model based on circles to explain and understand this seeming anomaly.

Try this test. Draw two circles on a piece of paper, one small and one large. The inside of the circle represents your knowledge (everything you know) about a single

For each of the subjects you are studying, draw three concentric circles. Place what you definitely know and are comfortable with in the inner circle (key words will do). Place those topics which you know about but which you are not quite on top of in the middle ring. Finally, place those topics which you are unfamiliar with or which you feel could be included to pick up extra marks in the final ring. You can now use this to prioritise your study and revision.

topic, or perhaps all the topics you have a grasp of. The outside represents all the knowledge that exists in the world about that topic or topics. The key part of the circle is its circumference, as this depicts how big the boundary is between what you know and what you don't know. The small circle represents someone who knows relatively little. In this case the boundary is small, and as a result there are few touch points between what the person knows and doesn't know. People with small circles of knowledge tend to be know-alls who think they have the answer to everything (or at least they have an opinion about everything despite not having a grasp of the topic under discussion). This is because they have limited awareness of how little they know and how much they don't know, and therefore don't feel motivated to learn anything new. And why should they, when they know everything? Contrast this with the larger circle. Here the knowledge boundary is much larger and the touch points between what is known and what is unknown are much more numerous, hence the feeling that there is so much more to learn. Such people are knowledge hoovers, always seeking to suck up everything they can learn to update and augment the knowledge they already have.

So now that you have got the gist of the idea, let's apply it to your study. The best way to do this is to take a subject and then draw three concentric circles. Each circle has a meaning, as follows:

Time management lies at the heart of being able to complete your exams and study with confidence. Clock the advice given in IDEA 12, *Tick, tock*.

Try another idea...

- The inner circle (exam readiness ring) is everything you know and are confident that if you were tested on it tomorrow you would be able to get most of it correct.

- The middle circle (needs more attention ring) is everything you are relatively happy with, but which you need to work on to get to the level of confidence you need for the exams.

- The outer circle (concerned ring) is everything you really don't know but ought to if you are to master your subject. This could also include additional topics which would demonstrate mastery of your subject.

Having defined each of the rings, populate each one with the topics and key words that cover the subject you are studying. When placing the key words in each of the rings it is important to be honest with yourself and, if anything, err on the cautious side. So if you think you are borderline, better to place it in the outer of the two rings. Once you have populated the rings, you can move the topics towards the centre ring as you get on top of them.

'The illiterate of the 21st century will not be those who cannot read and write, but those who cannot learn, unlearn and relearn.'
ALVIN TOFFLER

Defining idea...

Q   Could I use this as a motivational tool?

A   *Yes, you can. The best way to do this is to print it off as a slide, or better still, make it poster size if room permits. As you master the topics in the outer rings you can move them into the inner rings. When everything is in the central ring you can sit back comfortable in the knowledge that you have done as much as possible in readiness for the exam.*

Q   I can see its value for motivation, but what about prioritisation?

A   *Now you come to mention it, it could serve that purpose too. Once you have placed all the topics in their respective rings you can then determine which topics are the most important and plan your study accordingly. You can also combine the circle model with past papers, as this will allow you to cut out those topics which are less likely to appear in the exam.*

Q   Any other uses for the model, given it's such a good one?

A   *The final use that springs to mind is connecting related topics together. This can be very helpful because it will show you which topics should be studied together and it could also help you prioritise too. The way to do it is to draw lines between the connected topics in your model and then make sure you study them together.*

43

Smash, bang, wallop

Science subjects usually require you to conduct a practical experiment as part of your exams. How can you prepare for this, as this is truly a test you can't second guess?

Practicals were always fun. Playing with dangerous chemicals, electricity, wave machines and bulls' eyes was a great excuse to mess around. The problem was that when it came to the practical exam, things got a little more serious.

Practical exams are very different from written exams. Preparing for your written exam is very easy in comparison because you can practise, use plenty of techniques to help you learn and regurgitate the material, and even get familiar with the types of questions you will have to answer. You can't revise for a practical exam in the same way because there's nothing to revise; it's about how you can deal with the conundrum on the day. I remember doing a physics practical exam at school and it all went horribly wrong. I had taken my time conducting the experiment, but when

Here's an idea for you...

Preparing for a practical requires you to have excellent planning skills. To give you the best chance of success, create a prompt sheet and memorise its contents. The prompt sheet should cover all four areas you will be examined on (planning, obtaining your evidence, analysing your evidence and evaluating your evidence) and pose questions to double-check that you have included everything.

it came to writing up my notes, I found that nothing made sense. My graphs were all over the place and I discovered that I had made a big error early on that invalidated everything that followed. It was too late to do anything about it. I wasn't happy, but fortunately my workings saved the day and I scraped a pass. I learnt a lot from that experience though, I can tell you. So, having looked into practicals in more detail, I can reveal to you now what a good one would look like. To get the maximum marks you will need to structure your answer along the following lines:

- Purpose – what is the point of the experiment and what are you hoping to find out? This is often best presented as a question or questions you are intending to answer.

- Apparatus – what equipment did you use? It is best to list this as it tends to look neater. You should also always include a diagram of the equipment with labels.

- Method – what approach did you to take to complete the experiment? This needs to be systematic and include as much information as possible. It may feel a bit silly, but the way to complete this is to imagine you are instructing someone who has never done anything like this before. You should also include any relevant knowledge of the subject under investigation, as this will pick up extra marks.

■ Results – what did you find? Results are best shown in a table, because it cuts down on the writing and presents the information in a neat and accessible way. If some of your results seem odd or even wrong you should draw attention to them. You won't be able to hide them, and at least it shows that you are aware of the anomaly.

Don't let stress get the better of you. Learn how to keep your calm and float over to IDEA 37, Don't panic!

Try another idea...

■ Analysis – what observations can you draw from the experiment? Sometimes it is a good idea to draw a chart, especially if you want to highlight any odd results.

■ Conclusions – what critical comments can you make about the experiment, the results and your analysis? This is an important part of the practical and you should cover such things as how you thought the experiment would turn out against how it actually did, what the results tell you and whether or not these are reliable, what other evidence (such as your knowledge of the subject) can be used to reinforce or question the results, and how you could improve on the experiment.

If you cover all the areas above, you ought to do very well.

Examiners are looking for you to demonstrate a number of things in your practical. These are:

'Keep your fears to yourself, but share your inspiration with others.'
ROBERT LOUIS STEVENSON

Defining idea...

■ Your ability to plan and execute the experiment in the allotted time.

- How you collected the evidence during the experiment.

- Your approach to analysing the results. Ideally you should use a combination of approaches, including pictures, graphs and descriptions.

- Your skill in evaluating the experiment, your approach, the evidence collected and the conclusions you draw.

Like all exams, if you can add further snippets of information about the subject of your experimentation, you will gain extra marks.

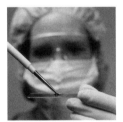  

Q **Is it really impossible to get help for practicals?**

How did it go?

A *Well, not entirely. Some examination boards have developed teaching guides for this type of exam, and especially those which include practicals as part of their coursework assessment. These guides are invaluable as study aids because they can tell you lots about how practicals are marked and how best to approach them, and best of all, they provide you with a few examples.*

Q **What if I realise I've gone down the wrong track?**

A *This can be a real problem. Above all else, you mustn't panic, as this won't help at all. The best thing to do is to follow your original train of thought and complete the practical in the allotted time. This will allow you to pick up marks for your approach. Unless you have discovered your error very early on, you shouldn't start again as it is unlikely that you will have time to complete everything and you'll be in such a rush that you'll probably make even more mistakes.*

Q **Can I retake practicals?**

A *Yes, you can. You normally have to leave it for six months or perhaps longer, depending on the examination board's rules. If you do retake, just be careful not to slip into the same problems you had first time round. Make sure you understand why you fouled up the first time and create a prompt sheet to cover all bases this time around.*

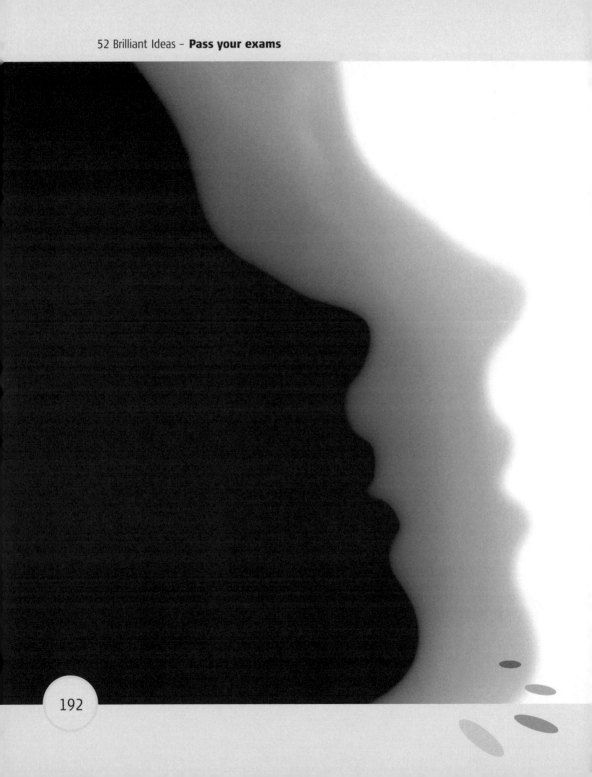

44

See, hear, feel

Have you ever thought about your learning style and how this affects your study and exam performance? Using your strongest sense makes most sense.

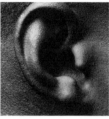

We all have five senses, but you won't get much revision done if you eat your notes or sniff them. Of the other three — seeing, hearing and feeling — we all have a favourite, and this can help maximise your studying skills.

So what are you then? Are you someone who prefers to think and talk in pictures? Do you love words and can pick up what people say very precisely? Or maybe you enjoy getting into the thick of the action and love the emotion of it all? The good thing is that you can tell what your sense of preference is quite easily, and once you know, you can fine tune your studying and revision techniques to maximise the benefits. If you are observant, you should notice that those around you use certain types of language and gestures most of the time. You should also notice that the speed at which they talk differs too. You will see some people who talk very fast, use words like 'see', describe things in a visual way and have their arms flailing

Here's an idea for you...

The next time you are discussing a subject get a friend to watch and listen to you. Ask them to note down the words you use, how fast you talk and the type of gestures you use. They should be looking out for any visual words, feeling words or words that remind them of sounds. When you have finished, ask them to read out the words you have used and give feedback about what they saw. At the end of the exercise you will know what preference you have.

everywhere – these are the visualisers. You will notice those who are much more considered in the way they talk; it's like they take time to choose the right words and use few gestures – these are the auditory types. Finally, you will bump into people who are even slower and will feel their way through everything. They will use language like 'let's kick that idea about' or 'I haven't got a good feeling about this' – these are the kinaesthetics.

So you know the types and you know which category you fit in; but how on earth does this help you with your studying? Well, first you need to ensure that you are playing to your sensory strengths from the start, which means right from the first class or lecture. Next, you need to apply your skills in the right way in the right context, in other words in class, when you are studying and when you are preparing for your exams. So here goes:

■ If you're the visual type, you'll need to underline key words and use different colours when capturing or emphasising your notes during lectures, and remember to use plenty of symbols and charts to bring it all alive. When reviewing your notes you should recreate them using images and symbols as much as possible, and when preparing for the exams you should attempt to recall the information in pictorial form. For this you'll need to work out where you can replace text with images. Most importantly, in the actual exams you'll have to make sure you can turn the images back into words.

If you want to get even more into your inner self then give IDEA 46, *The inner game*, a try and sort out the battle between Self 1 and Self 2.

Try another idea...

- If you're the auditory type, you'll need to make lists and key headings during your lectures, take every opportunity to discuss the topics you have learnt, use plenty of books and handouts, and even think about using a tape recorder to capture the lectures. When reviewing your notes you should write them out and read them out loud to yourself, summarise them into key words and consider group study, where you can discuss concepts with others. And finally, as you get nearer the exams, practise written papers, read your notes out loud (again) and make tapes of your notes to listen to.

- For the kinaesthetics amongst you, you should take every opportunity to attend field trips, practicals and get active. If necessary, you will need to do this yourself by converting what you have learnt into a real world experience for you. When it comes to study you should bring your notes alive by using real-world objects, like models, photographs and case studies. The exam prep is hardest for the kinaesthetic, so you will need to practise converting your real-world experience into the written word. Here it is a good idea to practise exam questions and knock the ideas around with a fellow kinaesthetic. One advantage you'll have is in all those real-world case studies – examiners love those.

'There are tones of voice that mean more than words.'
ROBERT FROST

Defining idea...

Q   I like this idea of using my senses; can I use it to good effect in the exams?

A   *You can, but remember that you will still need to answer the question in a traditional manner. So although you might have a strong visual preference, you won't be able to answer the question in pictures I'm afraid. But that shouldn't stop you from adding the odd illustration or two.*

Q   Can this technique help to influence the examiners?

A   *A good question. The problem you'll have here is that you won't know what the examiner's sensory preference is, and she will be working to a marking guide. That said, it's a good idea to mix all three sensory types into your paper (visual, auditory and kinaesthetic), as that way it'll appeal to any examiner. The interesting thing here is that they will latch on to those words above everything else, which should improve the perception of your paper.*

Q   I get the gist of this, but can you give some more words to help me?

A   *Of course. Visual words include sight, appear, view, survey, spotlight, highlight, glimpse, paint, show and imagine; auditory words include listen, sound, remark, report, rattle, mention, speechless, amplify, muffle and loud; and kinaesthetic words include touch, grasp, impact, kick, scrape, hunch, pressure, rush, smash and handle. Does this help?*

45

It's as simple as a, b, c

Multiple choice exams are more commonly known as multiple guess, given that most students think they are a breeze to answer. If only that were true!

I don't like multiple choice exams because:
(a) you have to revise everything just in case;
(b) you have little time to think about each question; or (c) the options always look the same.

Multiple choice exams are seductive because most students believe them to be much simpler than any other type of test. This belief stems from a variety of reasons, but the principle one is that the answer is in there and all you have to do is to pick it out from a list of wrong ones. If there are four answers of equal merit, you have a 25% chance of guessing it correctly, and if you can narrow the field even further, then you might get to a 33% or even 50% chance of getting it right. Ah, if only it were that simple. Guessing is always an option, but if you really don't know the subject, you don't know it. And examiners aren't going to make your life easy as they want to test your deep knowledge of the subject, which means that at least three answers will be somewhat right. Your job is to select the one that is most right! You in fact have to be much better prepared for multiple choices exams than

Here's an idea for you... **Get hold of as many past papers as possible and sit each one over a period of a couple weeks. After a while you will start to see familiar questions popping up, as examiners only have a limited number they can ask. With enough practice you will be able to recognise upward of 75% of the correct answers when you sit the exam, giving you plenty of time to focus on the unfamiliar ones.**

any other because they tend to cover a much broader range of topics and, unlike essay-based exams, you are less in control. Here are a few hints and tips to get the best marks possible:

- Obvious to say, but make sure you read each question and its answers through carefully before you go to guns. If you rush, it's easy to misinterpret the question and hence plump for the wrong answer.

- Some people prefer to read the question and think about what the answer could be before they look at the answers. For those students who know their stuff, this is a good strategy to adopt, because it helps them answer the question more rapidly.

- Eliminate those answers which are obviously wrong. This is best done by crossing them out so that you don't keep re-reading them.

- Sometimes the answer which is almost correct is placed before the real answer as a way of tempting the student to jump to an incorrect conclusion (sneaky).

- Statements that appear true can in fact mislead the student because although they may be true, they may not actually answer the question. In this case, it is a good idea to check back with the question to make sure the answer is indeed the right one.

■ Extra long options or those which seem to have more jargon are almost always the wrong ones.

In order to do well in all your exams, it's a good idea to develop your exam hall skills. So sit down and turn over to IDEA 38, *Exam hall excellence*.

Try another idea...

■ If a question ends in 'an', the answer should start with a vowel. In other words, look for the grammatical clue in the question, as this could make it easier to select the right answer. So if a question asked: 'The period between two ice ages is known as an...' the answer would need to begin with a vowel. In this instance, the answer to choose would be 'Interglacial'.

■ If any of the options includes catch-all statements such as always and never, they are nearly always wrong. Just remember, though, sometimes they could be right!

■ The option which differs in length the most from the others is often correct. So look carefully at the shortest and longest options (bearing in mind the earlier bullet point, of course).

I hope this brief heads-up on the nature of multiple choice exams has made you recognise that they are not such a breeze as you'd like to think. If you take care, read the question and use some of the hints and tips outlined above, though, you should do just fine.

'Between two evils, I always pick the one I never tried before.'
MAE WEST

Defining idea...

*How did
it go?*

Q **What's negative marking?**

A *This is where the examiner will deduct a mark for every question you get wrong. The purpose behind this is to stop students from randomly selecting the answer from the list. If you are faced with this situation, you are better off moving onto another question than making a wild stab at the answer. In other words, if in doubt, leave it out.*

Q **So should I always leave the question if I don't know the answer?**

A *No, because if negative marking doesn't apply, there's nothing to lose by having a guess. And remember, one answer is always so obviously wrong that you can ditch it straight away. And statistically, B or C are right more often; please don't ask me why.*

Q **What's the best strategy for answering this type of paper then?**

A *My approach is to make three passes at it. During the first pass you should aim to answer every question that you are 100% certain about. This will boost your confidence and avoid any panic that might set in if you start at question 1 and simply work your way through. In the next pass you should work on those questions where you are less confident but feel you can work the answer out. In the final pass you should mop up all the difficult questions and those you'll just have to guess.*

Q **Should I go back and change an answer if I think it is wrong?**

A *The general advice here is that if you thought you were correct when you answered it, you were probably right. Those who go back to change their answers normally change them to the wrong ones!*

46

The inner game

The golfers or tennis players amongst you may have come across a guy called Timothy Gallwey. A renowned sports coach, the secret of his success was that he perfected the inner game. So let's apply it to study shall we?

If you're anything like me, there's a little voice inside your head that's always nagging you about something, telling you what you should do and why you are going to screw up that exam paper.

Some people call it your conscience. I call it a pain in the neck!

It's a real drag, but apparently all our efforts to improve ourselves and our performance actually interfere with what we hope to achieve; but before you throw this Idea away, read on. The secret to realising our studying potential is to stop this nagging inner voice. The key, it seems, is to stop trying hard to learn and to trust in your capacity to do so. In other words, try to make the learning process a more natural one. Gallwey made a distinction between Self 1 and Self 2. Self 1 is the stern

Try to listen to your Self 1 giving you a hard time. It will be telling you what to do, how to do it and such like. Once you have tuned into Self 1, see if you can distract it so that Self 2 can get on with the job of studying. You never know, you might even get to enjoy it. I find the best way to distract Self 1 is to play some loud music. It will worry about the music whilst Self 2 gets on with its study.

know-it-all, who issues commands and judges the results produced by Self 2. This is the inner conversation that says 'You haven't finished those revision notes yet' or 'I really don't think you have prepared well enough for that oral exam tomorrow'. Self 1 is generally untrusting of Self 2. Self 2 is the more human self. Packed with natural potential, it has all the skills and capabilities to achieve most, if not all, things. Most importantly, it is Self 2 that includes our ability to learn. Unfortunately Self 1 not only prevents us from starting the learning process, it also continues to hamper us as we go through it. It's there trying to convince ourselves that we are not quite as good as we think we are and that we are not cut out to be good at study or exams. Self 1's undermining of Self 2 does nothing for our self-esteem, nor does it help us get down to the serious business of being successful in our studies. So you've guessed it: our ability to continue to develop and realise our potential depends heavily on our ability to limit the controlling Self 1 and allow Self 2 to carry out the tasks in hand in a calm and natural manner. So how do you tame your Self 1? Gallwey suggests three steps:

■ First, it is important to suspend the judgements that Self 1 makes because all they do is undermine our natural abilities. Key to suspending judgement is being able to focus Self 1 on some neutral but critical element of the study process. So, for example, you could get it to look at the length of the questions on the multiple choice paper whilst Self 2 focuses on choosing the right answer.

- Secondly, you've got to trust Self 2. The good thing about distracting Self 1 is that it frees Self 2 to naturally select those things which are most relevant to the task in hand. Trusting Self 2 to get on with the learning process leads to a virtuous circle of better results, better perceptions and a reduction in the internal noise from Self 1. Over time, it seems that Self 1 begins to trust Self 2.

To get the best out of learning it's a good idea to catch up with some of the latest models. If that's sounds interesting, dive into IDEA 39, Learning how to learn.

Try another idea...

- Finally, keep choice with the choice maker. This is all about setting your learning targets and the outcomes that you want from your study. This means letting Self 2 select what it needs, rather than allowing Self 1 to second guess.

This inner game stuff reminds me of the film *The Matrix*. At one point Neo found himself standing on the top of a tower block preparing to jump across a highway to a building on the other side. He stood there telling himself 'free your mind' over and over again, then self-doubt crept in (thanks, Self 1) and as soon as he launched himself off the roof he fell to the ground. Self 1 sucks, doesn't it? Still, the good news is that Neo finally tamed Self 1 and Self 2 saved the day. But I'm telling you the plot.

'It is the mind that maketh good or ill, that maketh wretch, happy or poor.'
EDMUND SPENSER

Defining idea...

Q   Are you sure this stuff works?

A   *Well it does in sport and it seems to work within the workplace. I know many people who have tamed their Self 1 to give their Self 2 the space it needs to be great at study and exams. The only way you'll find out is if you give it a try and don't let Self 1 put you off.*

Q   How will I know Self 2 is in control?

A   *Trust me, you'll know. When you are truly in the zone and are busy doing stuff, you'll notice that you just get everything done and your mind is quiet. No inner voice talking to you. You'll also lose all track of time and before you know it, hours would have slipped by.*

Q   How can I get Self 2 in control?

A   *One of the best ways I use is to distract it with music. For example, when I am writing, I distract my Self 1 with some loud punk and New Wave music, which keeps it happy (or at least occupied), whilst Self 2 can get on with converting my thoughts into text. Plus the music gets my blood pumping, which keeps my energy levels up.*

47

The killer question

Every exam seems to have one; no matter how well you've prepared, there is always a question that seems to throw you. Being able to get through the inevitable panic is vital, as is trying to produce some kind of answer.

Examiners say they never intend to fox you in an exam, but I'm not convinced. Sometimes you can be halfway through a seemingly seductive question only to discover that it's an absolute killer. All that time wasted for so few marks.

In order to maximise the number of marks you get in your exam papers it is always recommended that you answer the correct number of questions. Good advice if ever there was any. This is all well and good until you find yourself in front of a paper with a really nasty question, or one which you think you know what the examiners are looking for only to find out you don't. The former is just tough, because it's not obvious how you're going to answer it; the latter might be just down to your misinterpretation of the question. There is a third type of killer question and that's the one you've started only to find that your mind goes blank

Here's an idea for you...

In order to cope with the killer question, try the following visualisation technique. Imagine you are sitting in the exam and you open the paper to find it full of killer questions. As you look down, visualise the questions and watch yourself complete them. How did it make you feel? What did you do to stay calm? How did you answer the question? What made the question a killer? Using this technique will help you get used to the feelings you might experience and help you identify potential areas of weakness in your studying that might need to be addressed.

halfway through. I remember taking one paper about undersea resources. Because I had narrowed my revision to a small number of topics, I found myself faced with a whole raft of killer questions I couldn't answer! I made a good stab at a couple of them, but the third was appalling. What a disaster. This is not the only time where I have faced the problem of the killer question; in fact, I have faced all three types. So I feel in a good position to offer up some advice on how to avoid and cope with it should one appear in any of your exams.

To minimise your chances of coming up against the killer question, you will need to make sure that you are fully prepared. Apart from revising enough, the best way to prepare yourself is to analyse the types of questions that can come up, in terms of both the wording and the topics they are testing you on. Most exam questions use similar language and structure, so getting comfortable with it is a surefire way to reduce the risk. Knowing your subject also helps you to avoid the panic that sets in when you realise that you are left with a killer question to answer. But what if, despite all your preparation, you find yourself in that difficult place? From my experience, the following strategies help:

- Read the exam paper thoroughly to make sure that you haven't missed any questions that you would feel more comfortable answering. Under exam conditions it's very easy to misread questions and make rapid decisions about which ones to answer. Slow down and spend a few minutes to make sure that you have got the gist of all the questions before you start to panic.

You can get killer questions in maths papers, but if you show all your workings, they won't be quite so bad. The maths exam is presented in full detail in IDEA 40, *More can be more*.

Try another idea...

- Always tackle the questions you feel most able to answer first. The reasons for this are threefold. First, it builds your confidence. Secondly, it buys you some time. And finally, it avoids the natural panic that sets in when dealing with a question which you know you are going to do badly on.

- When faced with a killer question, take a few minutes to read and re-read it so that you fully understand what it is asking of you. Then list all the key facts that you have revised which you reckon might be relevant to the answer. Group these into some kind of structure, then, and only then, begin writing. This approach will stop you from launching into a panic-based regurgitation of anything that springs to mind and it ensures that your answer has a good structure to it. This way, you'll be getting a higher mark for the question than you'd have got if you'd just flapped at it. The key here is to remain as calm as possible. I know it's difficult, because you have the added pressure of time, but if you panic it will only get worse.

'No passion so effectively robs the mind of all its powers of acting and reasoning as fear.'
EDMUND BURKE

Defining idea...

Q   Should I not bother answering the difficult question?

A   *No matter how bad you might think the question is, or indeed how awful
your answer might be, my advice to you is that you should always answer
it. Even if your answer only contains one or two of the major points, you
will pick up some marks. And when faced with this situation, every little
helps.*

Q   If I screw up the killer question will I fail?

A   *No, not always. If you have two good answers under your belt it is unlikely
that a badly answered third one will cause you to fail – so long as you
attempt it, of course. In some instances where everyone does badly
(remember, one man's killer question can be another woman's killer
question too), the marks are re-baselined to allow the right number of
students to pass at each of the grades. This has happened to me on a few
occasions, which was a relief.*

48

Open and shut case

Open book exams: you can take into them all the reference books you need or can carry. Sounds an easy way to pick up marks, but they can be quite deceptive. And it's another skill area that you'll need to hone.

I had to take an open book exam in my first degree. The exam was due to last up to six hours, but with some careful preparation I completed it within five and still passed with flying colours.

I think open book exams are a great idea because they avoid the usual problems of trying to recall lots and lots of information. You are normally allowed to take in all the materials you require to answer the questions (though tutors are usually forbidden) and use them as you feel fit. This can work to your advantage so long as you know your way around it all. Here are some hints and tips:

- Do your homework. This might seem a bit odd, given that you will have plenty of material in front of you, but it is an excellent idea to know what the exam will expect of you and what areas it will cover. This will allow you to bring the

Here's an idea for you... **Get a sample open book exam and, under exam conditions, answer one question with no preparation. Use as many books, notes and articles as you need. Note how you felt, how easy it was and so on. Spend the next day or two working through your notes, books, etc., marking them up to make access to the key facts easy. Then answer the question again, noting how you felt, etc. You should notice a distinct improvement in performance – which should tell you that open book exams are not as simple as you may have thought but that you can prepare for them.**

right books and papers into the exam rather than everything you can think of or carry.

■ Know your way around the material you are bringing into the exam hall. It is easy to waste valuable minutes trying to find your way around a textbook, or locating that wonderful example to support your argument. This only serves to build up the stress levels and could introduce silly mistakes into your answer. I find the best way to avoid all this is to mark up the key facts, figures, concepts and examples with highlighter pens and then add page markers so that you can access them quickly. I also find it very helpful to use coloured tags in order to categorise the information. This tends to make access even more rapid. If you find that you have lots of tags, then why not create an index at the front of the book to help you navigate once you're in the exam?

■ Create model answers. In exams where you will be required to answer mathematical questions it is a good idea to build up a folder with sample answers marked up for reference. I tend to use real questions from past papers.

The sample answers should show all the steps and working out. They should also be easy to follow, so that the basic approach can be applied with ease during the exam. If you are dealing with complex maths, then another idea which I have used to good effect is to build an approach you can follow. So this way, rather than worrying about the content of the answer, you can focus on following the method through which the answer is derived. In addition, you might want to write yourself some notes to help explain the approach so that you don't lose confidence during the exam. And finally, use a different colour to describe the approach – it really helps.

If you want to depart from the mainstream, then take a peak at IDEA 49, *Hidden messages* – it's out of this world!

Try another idea...

- Check your approach with your tutors. This is particularly important if you will be answering mathematical questions as you may have answered your sample answers incorrectly. I had mine checked out for a major exam (the one I mentioned above) a couple of days before the exam and guess what? One of them was completely wrong! A quick bit of rework was required and it paid off. So if in doubt, check it out.

'It's not what you know that matters, it's knowing where to get it that counts.'
ANONYMOUS

Defining idea...

So there you have it, an open and shut case, as Sherlock Holmes would say. And if you are well prepared, your open book exam should be a breeze.

How did it go?

Q **Surely, if it is an open book, I don't have to put as much effort in, do I?**

A *On the contrary, preparation is even more important for this type of exam because it is so easy to lose precious time trawling through pages and pages of text whilst trying to find that one example. Also, don't leave it to the last minute, as marking up your notes takes time and requires a lot of thought.*

Q **What should I take into the exam?**

A *This really depends on what you are comfortable with. If you prefer to take in textbooks, then go with that. If you prefer your own notes, then bring these in. It doesn't really matter what you bring in so long as you are familiar with it. You certainly don't want to be looking at it for the first time when you are answering the question.*

Q **Should I be aiming to finish the open book exam as quickly as possible?**

A *No. Like all exams, you should be comfortable that you have answered all the questions to your own satisfaction. Naturally, if you apply the principles set out here, you may well find that you finish early, and if you are do and you are happy you have covered everything, you are normally permitted to leave.*

49

Hidden messages

If you really want to try something completely different when it comes to studying, then look no further than subliminal learning. Maximum effect, mimimum effort? Sounds perfect.

We all know about subliminal messages being used in advertising, but can they work with studying? Some swear by subliminal learning, and there's all sorts of stuff on the internet designed to help you learn things without even trying. Bye, bye revision notes.

So, subliminal learning – what is it? Very simply, it is the process through which we can learn subconsciously. Yes, you heard it right, subconsciously. Apparently you can be doing any other activity whilst learning in this way. There is no requirement to read your notes, books or in fact anything remotely studious. So you could be watching your favourite television programme and still be learning, or even be asleep in bed. Now how fantastic is that? It's a lazy student's charter. You can slope

If this type of revision appeals to you, give it a try using one of the many products available on the internet. Order a tape and see what happens. There is a huge range of topics you can choose from. These include learning different languages, thinking positively and becoming a better salesman. There are even those that deal with relationships – if you happen to have problems in that area! If it works, incorporate it into your revision. If it doesn't, at least you haven't lost sleep over it.

around all day whilst subconsciously listening to all those subliminal messages and then walk into your exams and get straight As.

Now for the scientific bit. Scientists believe that your conscious mind is your awareness in so far as it allows you to take decisions, reason, think, communicate and plan. All the information it has to process has to come from somewhere though, and that somewhere is your subconscious mind. You can look at it as a vast library of everything you have ever learnt, as well as those pre-programmed behaviours and responses over which we have little control – instinct. The subconscious mind is capable of taking in everything we experience, from our birth onwards. What's so amazing about this is that it is capable of organising this information ready for future use and, most importantly, is able to make sense of it all and establish patterns of thinking which we then apply with our conscious mind. The fundamental difference between our two minds is that whereas the conscious mind is able to select and deselect information, the unconscious mind accepts everything that is sent to it. The reason why subliminal learning can be so powerful is because it interacts directly with the subconscious mind, which will take everything at face value without making any rational judgements. The tapes and products you can buy are all designed to do just that. If the messages are powerful they can actually change how you behave.

If you don't believe anything I have just told you, then you might like to hear about some research undertaken by a group at the University of Boston. A team of scientists got a bunch of students to perform a task whilst subliminally training them to do another. Whilst they were working on their allotted task, a series of dots were moving randomly across their computer screens. This apparent randomness was nothing of the sort, as one in 20 was moving in a particular direction. When they were later asked to detect similar dots moving in the same direction they were able to do so to a much higher degree of accuracy than other students who had been trained in the task but had not been exposed to subliminal messages.

A major skill that is lacking in most students is the ability to think critically. If you want to develop these skills, then pay attention to IDEA 41, _Let's get critical._

Try another idea...

'Man's mind once stretched by a new idea, never regains its original dimension.'
OLIVER WENDELL HOLMES

Defining idea...

Q I like the sound of this subliminal learning thing. Where can I find more?

How did it go?

A *There is a wealth of websites which offer you the chance to learn subliminally. Of course you have to part with some cash, but hey, if it saves you hours of revision then it could well be worth it. You can buy tapes or software which runs on your PC flashing up messages which you can't see but your subconscious mind can, so you can be working whilst you absorb the messages.*

Q   What if they don't have the type of information I need? What can I do?

A   *Don't worry; you can create your own tapes which you can use for your revision. This will require you to undertake some work up front to distil the key messages from your notes and then record these onto a tape. It might not be as professional as those you can buy from the internet, but you can play them whilst you are asleep.*

Q   Does that mean I can give up my normal revision then?

A   *I wouldn't recommend it. Although subliminal learning has been proven to work, the experts believe that it cannot replace more active types of learning. But give it a go, as it's a great way to catch up on your sleep whilst burning the midnight oil revising!*

Q   I'm a nervous type; can subliminal techniques help me become more confident?

A   *Yes, I believe they can. There are numerous tapes available which will feed you positive and affirmative messages by telling your subconscious mind that you are strong and confident. Go on tiger, give it a try.*

50

Leave the scalpel behind

What's done is done. You can't go back into the exam hall and change your answer once you've left, so there's little point trying to dissect it and guess how you've done. But I bet you do.

It's funny, isn't it? You've just spent three hours concentrating, writing, worrying and getting cramp in your hand, and all people want to do is dissect every question and compare the size of their answers.

I'm sure you've been there. You have walked out of the exam hall, met up with your friends in the mood for some post-examinatory rest and relaxation, and rather than talking about doing something to unwind, you end up in some tortuous debate about how you answered question 1. Or the other classic which I always got was 'How well do you think you've done?' Most of the time I said I didn't know, which was probably a lie, but it usually did the trick. Well, apart from my parents, who would continue to push. Unless you are supremely confident about your exam technique and knowledge of your subject, it is unlikely that you could accurately predict your results.

Here's an idea for you...

The next time someone comes up to you after an exam try one or more of the following responses:

- **'Oh, I know I answered all the questions well, so there is no need to discuss them any further.'**

- **'I'd love to dissect the question, but quite frankly I can't see the point.'**

- **'Are you worried that you've failed? It's a bit late for that.'**

- **'I prefer to wait for the examiner to tell me how well I've done – unless, of course, you are the examiner.'**

I can understand the fascination: you've just spent the last *x* years studying the subject, you've stuck with it through thick and thin, you feel a little attached to it – heck, you've even bonded with it – and you don't want to let it go. Be that as it may, the dissection problem, as I like to call it, is unhelpful for a number of reasons. First, it stops you from putting the exam experience behind you. So if you have had a bad one, the last thing you feel like doing is reliving it over and over again with your friends, your teachers and your parents. Secondly, you can't actually do anything about it, so time spent on analysing what you have done is a waste. Thirdly, it can seriously undermine your confidence, even if you are feeling quite confident. If you start talking to someone who has answered the same question differently you begin to query what you did, and before long you have built an entire scenario of you screwing up the question. This can be particularly bad if you feel the person you are discussing it with is likely to do better than you. And finally, it can distract you from focusing on the next exam, which all your energy and positive thinking needs to be directed to. In the end it is a waste of time, so just say no.

Another interesting thing I have noticed over the many years I have been taking exams is the inverse relationship between how you feel the exam went and the mark you end up with. I always remember the English Literature exam I took at school. I and a couple of my friends were no great fans of the subject, especially as we had to do poetry and Shakespeare. The rest

Success in the exam hall is all about confidence, and if you have this then you have all the power you need to succeed. IDEA 19, *The power of positive thinking*, can show you where to get it from.

Try another idea...

of the class were keen students all desperate to do well. Anyway, the exam was really hard and the three of us came out thinking blimey, that was bad. Everyone else came out from the hall saying what a breeze the exam had been. We couldn't quite understand what was going on; had they sat the same paper? When the results came, we were the only ones to pass! So out of 30 students, the three most likely to fail passed. Obviously the inverse law was at work. It goes like this:

The perceived difficulty of an exam is inversely proportional to the grade you will achieve.

As a rule it seems to work, because all exams should challenge you. If you believe it was easy you will have probably missed something, so you ought to worry. Of course, if you have failed to prepare properly or haven't mastered your subject, then the hard exam will result in a poor mark. The law is not universal, but is a good rule of thumb for those of us who prepare well.

'Don't bother to be better than your contemporaries or predecessors, try to be better than yourself.'
WILLIAM FAULKNER

Defining idea...

How did it go?

Q **I really feel the need to figure out how well I've done; what can I do?**

A *Well, if you really must work out if you have done okay, my suggestion is that if (and this is a big if) you can take your exam paper away with you, you can use your revision notes to check whether what you wrote as your answer was about right. Even then it is unlikely that you'll be able to work out how you have done precisely, but if it eases you mind, then go for it.*

Q **How can I avoid the impulse to discuss the exam?**

A *I firmly believe that if you have prepared well for the exam you won't need to discuss it. After all, you will have a good idea if it was an okay paper and you answered the questions to the best of your knowledge and ability. If you believe you have done your best, then the result you get will be the result you deserve.*

Q **Any other advice?**

A *Go out: watch a film, go for a coffee – or something stronger, if you prefer. You need to take your mind off the exam and clear you mind, so do something that will distract you for a few hours and make sure you get some rest before getting ready for the next one. You will feel better.*

51

Vocation, vocation

The smart ones amongst us recognise that our learning does not stop once our formal education finishes. But the type of learning changes from being primarily academic to becoming more vocational.

It seems these days that if you stop learning you die (certainly the converse is true). Indeed, this has been shown to be true amongst the elderly. Throughout our careers we have to constantly reinvent ourselves and learn and apply new skills.

The rise of the vocational qualification is a trend that reflects the need to maintain our currency, but this requires a different set of skills to the ones we may have used in the past.

I have taken many vocational exams in the past, and I fully suspect I shall take a few more over the next 10–15 years. From taking the professional exams which allowed me to become a chartered surveyor, following courses in IT to allow me to get involved with technology projects, gaining a professional qualification in project

If you are following a vocational course and working at the same time, keep a logbook of examples of how you will be able to apply the skills you are learning to your job. This will help you in two ways. First, it will make what you are learning feel very real, and secondly, it will help you apply the skills you have learnt more easily when you are back in the office.

management and latterly in management consultancy, my reinvention never seems to stop. Tiring as it is, I have little choice, and increasingly, neither do you. Vocational exams differ quite a bit from the academic courses you will have taken in the past. The major departures are:

- They are much narrower than academic ones. Whereas academic courses are designed to cover subjects broadly, the vocational course is designed to cover a narrow subject to a much greater depth of understanding. In some cases, they can be very narrow indeed.

- Many vocational courses have a significant impact on your career progression because they lead to a professional qualification. For example, if you are an accountant it is likely that you will undertake some kind of study to become professionally qualified, and if you pass you will be able to do more interesting work and get paid more for doing it (surely the only objective in accountancy?). In some of the bigger firms you can be sacked if you fail your exams. How about that for exam stress?

- Vocational courses are designed to make you more competent at a subject. As a result they are often practical and you will be expected to apply the skills directly after completing the course. I believe that academic courses are there to broaden your mind whilst vocational courses are there to deepen your competence and expertise.

- Whereas you tend to study for academic courses in your teens and early twenties, most vocational study is undertaken once you are in work, and hence in your twenties, thirties, forties…

Have you ever given cram school some thought? In some parts of the world they are all the rage. If you're interested, then delve into IDEA 20, *Cramming until you drop*.

Try another idea…

- Vocational courses tend to be shorter, often lasting only a few weeks, and so your study is concentrated over a much shorter time frame. If it ends in an exam, you will have less time to revise, so this means that your study skills have to be in tip-top condition.

So what are the skills you need to succeed in vocational study? First and foremost is the ability to listen, interpret and apply what you have learnt to real-world situations; it's practicalities, not theories, that count in this kind of course. Secondly, you will need to be able to get to the point far more quickly in any exam because the subject matter is much narrower than what you might have been used to. The questions you will be set will be more direct and they will expect a direct answer. Thirdly, you will be expected to draw on your own experience to a much greater degree than in your early years of studying. And finally, the nature of the course will involve a lot more time thinking through particular problems and case studies, so there will be a need to interact a lot more, work in teams and apply what you have just learnt almost immediately. Vocational study is much less passive than academic courses.

'What we have to learn to do, we learn by doing.'
ARISTOTLE

Defining idea…

225

How did it go?

Q   What sort of vocational courses should I take?

A   The best way to figure out what vocational course is right for you is to consider your career needs. If you have a long-term plan, assess your learning requirements against that. You might also want to place it into a broader lifelong learning agenda if you have one.

Q   And I do that how, precisely?

A   If your employer provides this kind of service then all the better, because they will have HR professionals to help you assess your career goals and will usually have courses that match your career trajectory. Of course, most employers don't have that kind of thing, so you'll have to think about the skills you want to develop and then pursue a course that is able to give you them. The best way to do this is to carry out a skills assessment.

Q   Do professional qualifications matter that much these days?

A   It all depends. I have a number of professional qualifications which I no longer need. They were important at the time because they opened doors. I feel that professional qualifications are important where you have to demonstrate a level of expertise that is otherwise difficult to show, or where regulation requires it. So if you want to be a lawyer, accountant or surveyor, you will probably need a professional qualification. In some instances they don't matter at all, but at least they make you look important.

Don't worry, be happy

Sometimes things just don't work out when it comes to exams...despite all the hard work, your grade disappoints. The key thing is to figure out what to do next.

There is nothing like the feeling of waiting for your exam results: the beating heart, the dry mouth, the trepidation. Then you get the results and your feelings change dramatically.

If you've done okay, there's a feeling of 'Well, is that it, then? What next?' If the results are not quite so good, you'll feel more negative, but whatever you do, don't panic.

No one likes getting a mark or grade lower than they hoped for, but it's a fact of life when it comes to taking exams. Apart from the few naturals out there who seem to get the A grades with only the minimum of effort, most of us have to come to terms with the fact that we are good at some subjects and not so good at others. We also have to accept that, as much as we'd like to, we cannot expect to get the top marks in everything we do. Even though these comments might provide some comfort, there will be times when your grades disappoint because they don't meet the entry requirements of your selected university or profession. Indeed, only recently my

If you find yourself with grades lower than you'd hoped for, try a self-coaching approach, which can help you take something positive from the whole experience. Use the following questions to help coach yourself to a positive mindset and develop your response:

- What can you learn from this?

- What could you do to shift from where you are now to where you want to get to?

- What alternatives are available?

- Who might be able to help you?

- What will be your next action?

12-year-old son came home with a D for a biology exam he took (somewhat early!). He was upset because he was one mark short of a C. I explained to him that his dropped mark had not brought the world to an end, and besides, he was still very young. It was a useful experience and one from which he learnt a lot, and he is keen to retake the exam even though he doesn't have to because it is one module out of many. Contrast this with a good friend of mine at school who was delighted with his results, even though he failed. He came out from the headmaster's office and, with a broad grin across his face, shouted 'I've got three Fs!' The reason he was happy was that his new job only required him to sit the exams, not necessarily pass them. I am sure your response would have been quite different. Personally, I think he'd have been better off with the three Rs.

So, if the worst happens and your results fail to meet your expectations, what should you do? Before you take any action, it's important to consider the underlying reasons as to why your results were less than you had hoped for. So ask yourself whether the lower result was because you:

- were not prepared enough

- fell prey to exam nerves which then got the better of you

- left your revision far too late to be truly effective

- failed to answer all the questions

- failed to read the question correctly

- had too high expectations in the first place

If preparation is not enough, if all else fails but you don't want to, then consider getting a hired hand to help you through. See IDEA 21, *Hired hand*, for the gen on personal tutors.

Try another idea...

There are many reasons why you could have done badly, so I hope you won't just put it down to you losing your lucky rabbit's foot! Having established the primary reason, or reasons, you should then consider what lessons can be learnt from the experience and how they could help you approach the exam differently next time around (if there is a next time). This learning is the most important thing you can take away from the experience, because in the end the responsibility of learning is down to you and it is only you that sits the exam.

'Failure is the condiment that gives success its flavour.'
TRUMAN CAPOTE

Defining idea...

How did it go?

Q   Should I retake?

A   *This all depends on how important it is for you to get good grades. If the results are critical for university, and you still want to go, then the answer is yes, it probably is a good idea to retake. If they aren't critical, because you have been offered low grades to get in, then don't waste your time.*

Q   How quickly should I retake?

A   *Most examination boards tend to have set times for retakes, which is often six months after the main examination sessions. The decision of when to retake should be based upon two factors. The first is by how much you missed your desired grade: if the gap is small, you should retake it quite quickly; if the gap is large, you clearly have a lot of work to do so you'll need more time. The second is how confident you are that you covered the syllabus the first time around. Retakes rarely cover identical topics, so there is always a risk that you might fail again. Just make sure you take a long hard look at why you failed before deciding.*

Q   Should I worry about the long-term effects of the odd bad grade or two?

A   *Again, this very much depends on what career you want to pursue. In some cases, like law, accountancy and consultancy, your early exam results seem to count more than any degree – which I find crazy, given the demanding nature of many degrees. However, if you want a high-powered career, then you will need to either retake or set you career objectives a little lower.*

231

The end...

Or is it a new beginning? We hope that the ideas in this book will have inspired you to try some new ways of approaching your studies. Your pencils are sharpened and so is your mind, and you feel ready to tackle anything the examiners care to throw at you.

So why not let us know about it? Tell us how you got on. What did it for you – what helped you to nail that tricky essay or sail through the multiple choice? Maybe you've got some tips of your own you want to share (see the next page if so). And if you liked this book you may find we have even more brilliant ideas that could change other areas of your life for the better.

You'll find the Infinite Ideas crew waiting for you online at www.infideas.com

Or if you prefer to write, then send your letters to:
Pass your exams
The Infinite Ideas Company Ltd
36 St Giles, Oxford OX1 3LD, United Kingdom

We want to know what you think, because we're all working on making our lives better too. Give us your feedback and you could win a copy of another *52 Brilliant Ideas* book of your choice. Or maybe get a crack at writing your own.

Good luck. Be brilliant.

Offer one

CASH IN YOUR IDEAS

We hope you enjoy this book. We hope it inspires, amuses, educates and entertains you. But we don't assume that you're a novice, or that this is the first book that you've bought on the subject. You've got ideas of your own. Maybe our author has missed an idea that you use successfully. If so, why not send it to yourauthormissedatrick@infideas.com, and if we like it we'll post it on our bulletin board. Better still, if your idea makes it into print we'll send you four books of your choice or the cash equivalent. You'll be fully credited so that everyone knows you've had another Brilliant Idea.

Offer two

HOW COULD YOU REFUSE?

Amazing discounts on bulk quantities of Infinite Ideas books are available to corporations, professional associations and other organisations.

For details call us on:
+44 (0)1865 514888
fax: +44 (0)1865 514777
or e-mail: info@infideas.com

Where it's at...

Even more brilliant ideas...

Knockout interview answers

Ken Langdon & Nikki Cartwright

"One of us (Nikki) comes from the Human Resources angle. She has years of experience in summing up interviewees and making decisions on their character, their potential and their suitability for the job in hand. She knows what employers are looking for."

"One of us (Ken), being brilliantly qualified yet turned down after his first interview, began to think about the interview process and how he might have handled some of those tricky questions rather better. A business lifetime of asking and answering questions has helped him to perfect these skills." – **Ken Langdon and Nikki Cartwright**

Available from all good bookshops or call us on + 44 (0) 1865 514888

High-impact CVs

John Middleton

"Your CV should be the single most powerful weapon in your job-hunting armoury. It should hit a potential employer's desk and scream 'give me that job...!' Yet I must have looked at over 25,000 CVs in my time in various HR and personnel roles and most of them screamed 'bin me immediately...!' instead."

"The rest were either so dull that they sent me into a coma or so full of the almost godlike qualities of the applicant that I felt like returning them with a post-it note saying 'verily we are not worthy...'"

"So just think... If you hit all the right buttons with a potential employer, you can secure that sought-after job and at the same time help reduce the number of work days lost to comas annually!" – **John Middleton**